*America's*
# CHRISTIAN
HERITAGE

# *America's*
# CHRISTIAN
# HERITAGE

FIRST EDITION

*Crieve Hall Press*

Copyright 2017 Crieve Hall Church of Christ

Published by Crieve Hall Press, a ministry of Crieve Hall Church of Christ,
4806 Trousdale Drive Nashville, TN 37220
www.crievehall.org

Contributors:
*Steve Cantrell*
*Keith Ericson*
*Gary Hall*
*Andy Richter*
*Bill Watkins*

Editor: *Beverly Watkins*
Design & Production: *Jennie Pickens, Roger Blanton*

No portion of this book may be reproduced, stored in a retrieval system, or transmitted in any form or by any means – electronic, mechanical, photocopy, recording, scanning or any other – except for brief quotations in critical reviews or articles, without the prior written permission of the publisher.

Unless otherwise noted, Scripture quotations are taken from Scriptures from THE HOLY BIBLE, ENGLISH STANDARD VERSION. Used by permission. All rights reserved worldwide.

ISBN: 978-0-9994250-0-8

Printed in the United States of America

CONTENTS

*Introduction*

Chapter 1: *There is a God* — *11*
BY KEITH ERICSON AND BILL WATKINS

Chapter 2: *Is the Bible God's Word?* — *23*
BY GARY HALL

Chapter 3: *Is Jesus for Real?* — *59*
BY STEVE CANTRELL

Chapter 4: *God's Plan of Salvation* — *79*
BY ANDY RICHTER

Chapter 5: *A History of Christianity* — *91*
BY KEITH ERICSON

*Conclusion* — *105*

## INTRODUCTION

In order to understand our nation's Christian heritage we must first understand the Christian religion and determine how this religion can/does affect our lives and our nation's posture as we exist among all other nations on this planet. If we cannot identify the Christian religion, it's obvious we cannot identify our nation's Christian heritage.

So the first three chapters establish the basis for this book. We are not attempting to convert anyone to a set of religious beliefs as we look at the foundation for Christianity. However, a person may question his/her beliefs when reading about many religious practices that developed up through the centuries, practices that have no foundation in New Testament teaching.

The citizens of most nations adhere to a belief in Christianity to some degree. Exceptions are those nations governed by Islam, or nations whose people are followers of religions that rely on ancient traditions and ignore Biblical teaching.

But the people of most nations claim to believe in the Bible and in Jesus Christ as the Son of God. So it makes sense to take an in-depth look at how strong our beliefs are and how we are influenced by forces that would pull us away from our Christian beliefs.

Anyone who reads this book will understand that, without a doubt, there is a God, that He has authored the Bible and that Jesus Christ is His Son. The first three chapters contain abundant proof of these claims. Chapter four explains how God established His plan for a relationship with us and chapter five shows what man has done with God's plan up through the centuries.

A person who reads this entire book will understand that God did not abandon the human race as some tell us. There are some who claim that there is a creator but he turned us loose on this planet to do our own thing and to expect no rewards or punishment – that when we die, that is the end, there is no after life. They would say that Adolph Hitler, in spite of his cruel treatment of millions of people, finally took his own life and drifted off into eternal nothingness. They would also say that a person who lives a righteous Christian life will also die and that's the end, he/she had no soul and could expect no place in an eternal life with the God of this universe.

There are others who say God gave instructions to us through the Bible, but He leaves the interpretation up to us and whatever conclusions we reach are fine with Him. That belief will be questioned seriously by those who read "America's Christian Heritage".

Atheist openly tell us that there is no God and that everything on this earth is here by chance or accident. They also believe that no matter how complicated the design of the human body is, the design is the result of chance and accident through millions of years, that no matter how extremely complicated the design is, there is no designer.

No matter what your beliefs, it is our hope that this book will encourage people to think seriously about the direction our nation seems to be headed and whether we can/should call America a Christian nation. So read these five chapters and decide for yourself what you think about our Christian heritage.

CHAPTER 1

# *There Is a God*

BY KEITH ERICSON AND BILL WATKINS

Is it still reasonable to believe in the God of heaven? In 2002, Paul Geisert coined a new term for atheists. He called them "brights".[1] Other atheists quickly adopted the terminology. The term was chosen to sway people to accept their point of view by characterizing atheists as intelligent and reasonable and by implying that those who are believers in God are dim and unreasonable.

It might help to know that some of the brightest people on the planet are deeply committed to belief in God. Scientists and philosophers around the world are unapologetic about their faith in a supreme being. And there are good reasons for thinking as they do.

There are many different reasons to believe in the existence of God. Here are a few:

THE EVIDENCE OF DESIGN IN THE UNIVERSE

To state the case simply:
1. If the universe shows evidence of design, there must be a designer.
2. The universe shows evidence of design.
3. Therefore there is a designer.

In the words of the apostle Paul: "For the wrath of God is revealed from heaven against all ungodliness and unrighteousness of men, who suppress the truth in unrighteousness, because what may be known of God is manifest in them, for God has shown it to them. For since the creation of the world His invisible attributes are clearly seen, being understood by the things that are made, even His eternal power and Godhead, so that they are without excuse, because, although they knew God, they did not glorify Him as God, nor were thankful, but became futile in their thoughts, and their foolish hearts were darkened. Professing to be wise, they became fools..." (Romans 1:18-22)

There is evidence of design everywhere!

The human body is evidence of God's handiwork. Evolutionists claim that the body created itself, but they cannot answer the question "How did these body parts create themselves?" They just tell us that it took millions of years for these "miracles" to happen.

**Let's look a little closer, starting with the human heart**
The human heart is a muscle that beats about 70 times a minute. That beating causes blood to move to all parts of the body through arteries and veins, taking oxygen to the entire body and bringing carbon dioxide back to the heart, then to the lungs where it is exhaled. The body needs oxygen and must get rid of carbon dioxide. Oxygen is fuel and carbon dioxide is waste.

A fascinating event occurs where the oxygen-rich blood is exchanged for carbon dioxide. Throughout the body are microscopic "gas-exchangers" called capillaries. These microscopic parts perform an amazing feat. Somehow they are "programmed" to remove oxygen from the blood, deposit it in cells, and remove carbon dioxide from the cells and send it into veins where it is eventually removed from the body. The evolutionist cannot explain how these capillaries developed. He simply tells us that through millions of years they developed because they were needed. He tells us that there is no intelligence behind all of this development – it just happened because the process was necessary. He tells us they were needed, but cannot show us how this need was recognized.

**The heart feeds oxygen to itself.**
Something else happens as oxygen-rich blood leaves the heart. Since the heart is mainly a muscle, it also must have oxygen to continue beating. The aorta is the main artery emerging from the heart. But at the point where this artery emerges, smaller arteries branch off and take blood to the entire surface of the heart in order for the heart to continue beating. Without oxygen the heart cannot live, and when the heart quits beating the body dies. No evolutionist can tell us how the heart knew it needed this blood-flow to its surface. He will probably tell us that the heart somehow figured out this need and developed these special arteries. But it is interesting to note that if the heart was beating and didn't have these surface arteries, it would have died before it could form these arteries. These surface arteries had to be in place when the heart started beating.

**Evolution, a theory without rational thinking behind it**
The evolutionist hides behind his "millions of years" theory and expects us to fall in line with his thinking without asking intelligent questions. If we examine the body's senses we have even more reasons to question that "millions of years" theory. Let's go to the evolutionist's explanation that two non-living minerals banged into one another in that liquid called primordial soup. The atheist/evolutionist says that this earth was once a red-hot ball, way too hot for any life to exist. But as it cooled and that primordial soup developed, there were all kinds of minerals and debris floating on and under the surface. Then – a miracle! These microscopic things began bumping into each other and after some time had elapsed, a living cell came into being. Then creatures. And from that point evolution was in full swing and after a few more million years – BINGO – humans are inhabiting the earth.

**Our sense of vision**
Considering how the evolutionist explains our beginning, let's look

at our sense of vision. As we examine sight, it becomes quite apparent that much planning and designing had to take place in order for eyes to perform the way they do. It immediately becomes a mystery trying to understand how these early so-called evolving creatures "knew" they needed to see what was going on around them. But the evolutionist will explain that somehow a big gathering of complicated cells began associating and forming new things and one of these new things began absorbing light and somehow, through millions of years, evolving creatures began noticing what was surrounding them when these new light absorbing things began attaching themselves to evolving creatures.

Believing such a theory involves far more faith and far less evidence than the idea that there is a God who rules over the universe and rules over our lives. Take just a brief look at our sense of vision.

Just below our forehead are two similar openings called sockets and our eyeballs sit in these sockets. The eyeball is a sphere about one inch in diameter. The inside of this sphere is lined with over one hundred million photo receptors. Light enters the eyeball through the lens in the front of the eye. The light that the photo receptors receive is taken by the optic nerves to the back of the brain where it is interpreted. It is only then that we know what we are seeing. Obviously this is a continuous process. But it is more complicated than just what is explained above. The optic nerves take light images from the left side of each eyeball to the right side of the back of the brain and optic nerves take light images from the right side of each eyeball to the left side of the back of the brain. These two parts of the back of the brain interpret what the eyeballs have absorbed as light. This brief explanation of the sense of vision only scratches the surface showing how complicated vision really is.

Vision depends not only on the development of an eyeball, but also on the simultaneous development of a mechanism to hold the eye, and the simultaneous development of a delivery system to transfer the light signals into electrical impulses, AND the simultaneous development of an organism that can receive the impulses, translate them into an image, and communicate that image and its meaning to the one that it benefits. Any one of these factors developing without the others would mean that there would and could be no seeing. They make up an irreducible complexity. All are necessary at once or none can function at all.

## Lungs – no muscles, but they work day and night

Another miraculous event continually works to keep the human body alive – inhaling and exhaling. One feature of our lungs is probably not known by many people. The lungs have no muscles. When we inhale and exhale, we do so because a part of our brain "tells" the diaphragm and rib muscles to expand. The lungs sit inside the space that has just been enlarged, so the lungs expand, causing the action called inhaling. Another part of the brain signals the diaphragm and ribs to relax and the lungs are forced to exhale. We inhale and exhale all the time, awake or sleeping, but pay no attention to our breathing – it's all automatic.

## Chromosomes – God's thinking shows up loud and clear

Human cells are microscopic and very complicated. In all cells, except red blood cells, are parts called chromosomes, among many other things. Chromosomes contain a person's DNA and genes. There are forty-six chromosomes in each cell and they are arranged into pairs of twenty-three. But male and female reproductive cells only contain twenty-three chromosomes, only half as many as other cells. But when the male and female reproductive cells unite and a fetus begins to form, that fetus receives the twenty-three chromosomes from each parent giving this new life forty-six chromosomes, just like its parents. If the reproductive cells also contained forty-six chromosomes, the cells of the resulting fetus would contain ninety-two chromosomes and the next generation would contain one hundred eighty-four chromosomes. The next generation would have three hundred sixty-eight chromosomes. Do the math for ten generations!! The limiting of the number of chromosomes in reproductive cells is obviously necessary and cannot be attributed to chance or accident. It has to be by intelligent design from the creator of the human race.

**Denying God just doesn't make sense**

We wonder how an intelligent person can deny the existence of a creator when examining all of the overwhelming evidence that required intelligence and design to make just the human body what it is.

## THE VERY EXISTENCE OF THE UNIVERSE IS EVIDENCE OF GOD.

It is clear that the universe came from something rather than nothing. Stated as a simple argument:
1. Everything that begins to exist has a cause.
2. The universe began to exist.
3. Therefore, the universe has a cause.

If the universe has a cause of its existence, that cause must be a non-physical, immaterial being beyond space and time. Now there are only two sorts of things that could fit that description: either an abstract object like a number, or else an unembodied mind. But abstract objects can't cause anything. That's part of what it means to be abstract. The number seven, for example, can't cause any effects.

So if there is a cause of the universe, it must itself be uncaused, it must be timeless, it must be a transcendent, unembodied Mind, it must be vast, and it must be powerful beyond imagining.

Science now concedes that the universe had a beginning. In the words of the physicist P. C. W. Davies, *"the coming into being of the universe, as discussed in modern science . . . is not just a matter of imposing some sort of organization . . . upon a previous incoherent state, but literally the coming-into-being of all physical things from nothing."*[2]

Scientist Alexander Vilenkin, in his book, "Many Worlds in One: The Search for Other Universes" wrote, *"It is said that an argument is what convinces reasonable men and a proof is what it takes to convince even an unreasonable man. With the proof now in place, cosmologists can no longer hide behind the possibility of a past-eternal universe. There is no escape, they have to face the problem of a cosmic beginning."*[3] Since the universe has not always been, it had a beginning. In that it had a beginning, something must have caused it. We call that being God.

MAN'S MORAL NATURE IS EVIDENCE OF THE EXISTENCE OF GOD.
True morality comes from God. To state the case simply:
1. If God does not exist, objective moral values and duties do not exist.
2. Objective moral values and duties do exist.
3. Therefore, God exists.

**Morality is a sense of "oughtness"**
While morals can be mis-trained and untrained, it's a fact that humans have a sense of how the world ought to be and how they themselves ought to behave. There is nothing in the physical world that demands a moral code, and yet humans have such a code, whether they choose to live by it or not. Animals have no such sense of "oughtness." In fact nothing else in our world lives with such an understanding – only humans. Morality is not so much an understanding of how the world is as it is a sense of how the world should be. It lives in us – not with the force of an observation – but with the force of a command.

**Morality does not come from nothing.**
There are some things that can't exist unless something else exists along with them. Something cannot be carried unless there is something else that is carrying it. Something cannot be popular unless there are many people who like it.

Commands are like this – they can't exist without something else existing that commanded them. To put it another way, God is a moral being, and those who are made in His image are also moral beings.

**Every human feels the pull of morality.**
If someone morally ought to do something, then this overrules any other consideration that might come into play. It might be in my best interest not to give help to the needy, but morally I ought to, so in reality I ought to. It might be in my best interest to lie about being too busy to do a helpful deed on Saturday so that I can watch a ball game, but morally I ought not, so all things considered I ought not. If someone has one reason to do one thing, but morally ought to do another

thing, then that person understands he ought to do the other thing. Morality overrules everything.

**Commands are only as authoritative as the person that commands them.**

If I were to command everyone to pay extra taxes so that the government could give me more money, no one would have to do it. The reason is because I don't have the authority to issue that command. If, on the other hand, the government were to command everyone to pay extra tax so that we could spend more money on something, that would be different, because the government does have that authority.

Since morality has more authority than any human person or institution, morality can't have been commanded by any human person or institution. Since morality overrules everything, morality must have been commanded by someone who has authority over everything. The existence of morality points us to a being that is greater than any of us and who rules over all creation.

> *God is present everywhere and He's left his fingerprints all over creation. The earth is marked as if by a sign that declares in bold letters: "Made by God."*

GOD HAS REVEALED HIMSELF.
**He has revealed Himself in the world.**

In Psalm 19:1-4 David said, "The heavens declare the glory of God; and the firmament shows His handiwork. Day unto day utters speech, and night unto night reveals knowledge. There is no speech nor language where their voice is not heard. Their line has gone out through all the earth, and their words to the end of the world."

God is present everywhere and He's left his fingerprints all over creation. The earth is marked as if by a sign that declares in bold letters: "Made by God."

**He has revealed Himself in the Word.**
Look at verse 7 of Psalm 19: "The Law of the Lord is perfect, converting the soul..."

God has not only revealed Himself in a general sense through His creation of the world, but has also made known His character through His Word. The Bible is bursting with direct statements from God about God – and it reveals His mind, His heart, and His will for us.

**When we acknowledge Him, our response should be worship.**
Check out Psalm 19:14 - "Let the words of my mouth and the meditation of my heart be acceptable in your sight, O Lord, my Rock and my Redeemer."

There is so much more that could and should be said. There are so many sources of information that lead clearly toward the fact of the reality of our God. The resurrection of Jesus – which cannot be adequately explained apart from the existence of God, the prophecies of the Bible, the life, teachings, and fulfilled prophecies of Jesus all point to the same thing – God Is!

We need to begin at the starting point: "In the beginning, God created the heavens and the earth" (Genesis 1:1). No other explanation satisfies the facts and no other explanation satisfies our souls.

**Where do we go from here?**
The next parts of this book show that the Bible is God's word, that Jesus Christ is real and that God planned salvation for the entire human race before He even put Adam and Eve, our fore-parents, in the Garden of Eden.

When we look at how we humans have disregarded God's word over and over, we wonder how God can still love us and provide for our wellbeing. The truth is – there will be a judgment day and all of us will answer to the God of the universe. The more seriously we view life and our relationship to our creator, the easier it will be to face the end of life when that time comes.

"It is impossible to rightly govern the world without God and the Bible."

-GEORGE WASHINGTON

*For chapter 2 endnotes please see*
*www.americanchristianheritage.org*

CHAPTER 2

# *Is the Bible God's Word?*

BY GARY HALL

Now that we have established that God exists, the questions are: has He communicated with us and how? We could look at every book ever written claiming to be from God, but this would be unrealistic. Thus we will narrow our scope. In particular we want to see if the Bible is God's word, not God's word, or partly God's word. If the Bible is God's word, and not partly, then all other religions and their books are immediately excluded as being God's word for man since Jesus said in John 14:6: "I am the way, and the truth, and the life; no one comes to the Father but through Me."[1] This conclusion does not mean that the other books do not have some good things to say, but if a person comes to believe the Bible and to believe in Jesus then many other religions are not how God wants people to live today. This may sound harsh to some, but God is trying to show the world the true way to peace and love and joy- what all are looking for.

Now let's first look at what the Bible says about itself. Let us encourage you to read Exodus 24:3-4, Deuteronomy 30:9-10, Jeremiah 30:1-2, Matthew 22:23-33, Luke 1:1-3, John 10:35; 19:35, Acts 2:22, 1 Corinthians 14:37, 2 Timothy 3:16-17, 2 Peter 1:16; 3:15-16, and 1 John 1:3.

These verses are just some of the verses which claim that their words or books are from God or were witnessed by themselves or others to be true. This leaves us with two choices: either they are from God, or they are not. Thus we need to see if anything else indicates to us whether these writers are telling the truth or not about their writings being from God. We cannot deal with everything in one chapter, so we will try to hit some of what are considered the biggest arguments against the Bible.

The first area we want to look at is science and the account of the creation. Rather than deal with every question one by one, let's look at the creation account as a whole. First of all, while Bishop Ussher (James Ussher, 1581-1656) may have done very good, extensive research in trying to determine the date of the creation of the earth and in coming up with a date around 4000 B.C., the Bible was not written as a science book with every detail included. This does not imply that what the Bible says is incorrect; it just says that one who reads the Bible does not need to put in the Bible something that it does not say. Bishop Ussher used much extra-Biblical data, but he also used information from the Bible, as he interpreted it. His date may or may not be accurate concerning the age of the earth, but it is not a date that the Bible gives us per se. In other words, one cannot judge the accuracy of the Bible based, or at least solely based, upon the work of Bishop Ussher.

**A Young Earth or an Old Earth?**

For those who believe in a "young" earth (possibly validating Ussher's work), the Bible's account of how the universe was created fits very well. For those who do not believe in a "young" earth, whether because of science data they have seen or studied or for some other reason, let us give a couple of possibilities to fit that scenario. First of all it is not until the fourth day that God created the sun and the moon, the main instruments used in how we measure time. The question has to be asked then: how were a day and night kept in Genesis 1 even before day four? Some argue that since the same expression is used after day three as was used with the first three days, then it has to mean the same duration in terms of time, and since we have the sun and moon in day four that would imply twenty-four hour days for all seven days. First of all if we believe in an all powerful God, then we believe that He can create a universe "grown" as He did Adam (see Genesis 2:15). Thus God could have created the universe in six 24-hour periods, creating it as an "old" universe satisfying whatever science has discovered. Just a quick aside to this last possibility, some would argue that this idea of God creating a universe that looked "old" would go against His nature, but why? Again we have to emphasize the fact that in no way does God ever tell us how old the universe and/or the earth is. This is man's assumption.

**Look at the Hebrew word "Yom"**

Now another possibility to an "old" earth is how the Hebrew word "yom" is interpreted. Sometimes it means day, just the opposite of night (see Judges 19:8-9). Sometimes it is used as a representation of a twenty-four hour time period (see Exodus 20:9), and sometimes it means an indefinite long period of time (see Numbers 9:22 or Genesis 38:12). Many would also quote 2 Peter 3:8 which indicates that a day can be a long period of time (a thousand years). So again the question arises: does "yom" in each day of creation represent a twenty-four hour period or an undescribed period of time such as just the time to go from light to darkness and back again, however long that took? If the time within the first three days of creation is not limited to our present reckoning of time, could this not give ample opportunity for God to create the universe and the earth in whatever time period He wanted, even with a "big bang"? Even some Christians will be angry at this assumption saying that this idea automatically leads to man evolving from a single cell, but that is a false assumption. There are many Christians who believe in God's creating the universe over a period of extended time, but do not believe in this unproven form of the theory of evolution. Also believing in the "Big Bang" Theory does not exclude God because God, in this theory, would be the One who created the matter in the first place and caused it to explode and made sure that the pieces went where they were supposed to go.

### Science and the Bible do not conflict each other.

We have not picked one of these theories over another on purpose. We have shown that the Bible does not have to contradict these different ideas of creation. Therefore the argument cannot be used to say that the Bible is wrong and thus not from God. Again we will state this very important concept one more time: if a person has come to the idea of an all-powerful God, then that God can make the universe/earth however and over what period of time He wants, whether literal twenty-four hour days or longer periods of time. Before we leave Genesis 1, some will bring up the dinosaur question, saying that they existed, but where are they in the Bible? We reiterate that the Bible was not written as a science textbook, so the Bible was not written to explain when the dinosaurs lived and for how long. Thus one cannot argue that the Bible is inaccurate because of the dinosaurs. There is a possibility in Job 40:15-24 that the behemoth therein described is a dinosaur, but it also could be a hippopotamus; we just do not know. These past ideas are examples of man's interpretation of what the Bible says. What it says and does not say can cause misunderstandings of what the Bible says.

Let us stay in the area of science (even though the Bible is not a science textbook!), and look at some clear evidences of what the Bible does tell us.

In 1915, Richard Launcelot Maury wrote a paper entitled "A Brief Sketch of the Work of Matthew Fontaine Maury." The following is an excerpt from the introduction:

*"When I took charge of the Georgia Room, in the Confederate Museum, in Richmond, Virginia in 1897, I found among the De Renne collection an engraving of the pleasant, intellectual face of Commodore Matthew Fontaine Maury, so I went to his son, Colonel Richard L. Maury, who had been with his father in all his work here, and urged him to write the history of it, while memory, papers and books could be referred to; this carefully written, accurate paper was the result.*

*At one time, when Commodore Maury was very sick, he asked one of his daughters to get the Bible and read to him. She chose*

*Psalm 8, the eighth verse of which speaks of "whatsoever walketh through the paths of the sea," he repeated "the paths of the sea, the paths of the sea, if God says the paths of the sea, they are there, and if I ever get out of this bed I will find them."*

*He did begin his deep sea soundings as soon as he was strong enough, and found that two ridges extended from the New York coast to England, so he made charts for ships to sail over one path to England and return over the other.[2]"*

This same Commodore Maury read Job 28:25 and discovered "the weight for the winds".[3]

These two examples are given to show that nothing in the Bible contradicts what we know to be the laws of Physics or the like (of course the exceptions are when God is involved since our God can do anything He wants since He created it all). Likewise we could quote Isaiah 40:22 ("vault" or "circle" depending upon the translation) and Proverbs 8:27 which talk of the shape of the earth in terms of a circle long before anyone ever believed the earth to be round rather than flat. We could also quote Job 26:7 where he states that the earth hangs on nothing again contradicting the beliefs of man at that time (many believed either a supernatural being was holding the planet up or that it was in some ocean or on some creature's back). And what about Genesis 13:16; 15:5, and Jeremiah 33:22 which talk about the number of the stars being great (innumerable as the dust of the earth) when the ancients thought that there were under 3000 stars at the most (150 B.C. or even as late as 150 A.D.) until the invention of the telescope. While theories may come and go, we see that science and the Bible do not conflict!

### Was there really a flood?

Now that we have briefly (briefly is a good word because there is much written about science and the Bible. One just has to be sure that he/she is looking at what the Bible says and not what a man thinks it says) looked at science and the Bible, let us look briefly at the claim that history does not back up the Bible's claim that it is from God and thus inaccurate. We will start with the flood. Some have said that there was no earth-covering flood. Yet the evidences of the flood do exist. One such evidence is the fact that many ancient cultures have a story of a flood, for example "The Epic of Gilgamesh." While this story does not correlate exactly with the Biblical account of course, it tells of a flood such as in Genesis. This story comes from the ancient Mesopotamian region. While one could argue that one story was made up and all these other stories were derived from the one, it is also easily plausible that all of these stories came from one true event. There are archaeological/scientific discoveries to back this up, such as possibly Robert Ballard's discovery of evidence pointing to some catastrophic event happening to the Black Sea some 6000-7000 or more years ago. This catastrophic event was a large flood, at the least in that region. Even though Ballard does not believe in the flood as the Bible describes, he still believes something did happen (Robert Ballard is the one who is famous for hunting down the Titanic wreck).

**Historical accuracy of the Old Testament**

Concerning the historical accuracy of the Old Testament, we have "The Taylor Prism" backing up the Biblical account of Sennacherib's siege of Jerusalem in 2 Kings 18-19, 2 Chronicles 32, and in Isaiah 36-37. We also have "The Cyrus Cylinder" documenting Cyrus's allowing Babylonian captives to return home as is in Ezra 1:1-3 and 6:3. Likewise "The Black Obelisk of Shalmaneser" depicts Jehu and Shalmaneser living at the same time (Jehu is giving an offering to Shalmaneser). The Bible also has them as contemporaries. "The Moabite Stone" mentions Mesha, a king of Moab (see 2 Kings 3) but also mentions Yahweh. "The Tel Dan Stele" validates 2 Kings 8:28-29 telling of Hazael's victory at Ramoth-Gilead. The Ebla tablets validate the existence of the five cities mentioned in Genesis 14 and by the way in the exact same order. The excavation of Jericho shows that the walls of the ancient city fell somewhat outward which first of all is unusual since one would predict the opposite to happen with an enemy attacking from the outside and which actually matches Joshua 6:20. Abraham's name appears in Babylonia around the time that the Biblical Abraham lived. At one time some said that the laver of brass (bronze) during the time of Moses (Exodus 30:17-21) came from a time far past the time of Moses, but archaeological evidence has been found of such bronze lavers dating back to 1500-1400 BC, the same time as Moses. The Tel el-Amarna Tablets confirmed that Palestine had been captives to Egypt and Babylon, confirmed that the Canaanites and the Hebrews had been enemies, and confirmed the name of Jerusalem.

> *While theories may come and go, we see that science and the Bible do not conflict!*

**Historical accuracy of the New Testament**

To consider the historical accuracy of the New Testament, we start with the Roman census around the time of the birth of Jesus in Luke 2:1-8. Archaeological finds tell us that this census for taxation was started by Caesar Augustus and matches the years around when Jesus was born. Also an Egyptian papyrus tells people to go back home for the enrollment for such census. At the same time we have found evidence that Quirinius was governor of Syria around the same time validating Luke 2:2. Many believed that Luke was wrong in Acts 14:5-6 when he implied that Lystra and Derbe were in Lycaonia but Iconium was not because it went against what Cicero seemed to believe. It turns out that discoveries have shown that Iconium was a city of Phrygia for years, even centuries. A stone was found in the ruins of Corinth with an engraving mentioning Erastus; the stone dates back to about the time of Erastus the city treasurer of Corinth mentioned by Paul in Romans 16:23. Also in Corinth inscriptions have been discovered that tell of the existence of a synagogue there (Acts 18:4-7) and the meat market (1 Corinthians 10:25). Some used to think that Luke used the wrong word to say that Philippi was a "part" or "district" of Macedonia, but archeology has shown that this word was used at that time to divide the districts. Similar circumstances have validated Luke's use of "first man of the island" in Acts 28:7.

The "pavement" during Jesus' trial mentioned in John 19:13 has been discovered. Likewise the "Pool of Bethesda" only mentioned in John 5:2 has now been discovered. The same story is true for the Caiaphas and Sergius Paulus finds.

There are many other archaeological evidences of both testaments, but a summary of these last few paragraphs can be given by the following quotes:

*"No doubt archaeologists- adhering to the historical-critical method- will continue to present historical reconstructions that contradict key events described in the Bible. However,... the alleged problems with biblical history most often lie with humanly-contrived methods rather than the text. Further, there is only so much archaeology can do. It can neither prove, nor disprove, that a transcendent God has broken into history in demonstrative ways. ... that there is impressive evidence that biblical authors accurately described, and artistically presented, the historical events that they ascribed to God.*

*On the whole, however, archaeological work has unquestionably strengthened confidence in the reliability of the Scriptural record. More than one archaeologist has found his respect for the Bible increased by the experience of excavation in Palestine."*
-Millar Burroughs of Yale

*"As critical study of the Bible is more and more influenced by the rich new material from the ancient Near East we shall see a steady rise in respect for the historical significance of now neglected or despised passages and details in the Old and New Testament."*
-William F. Albright.

## Is today's Bible the same as the original text?

Now some will ask the question, "how can we be sure that the Bible we have today is what was originally written and not edited at a later date to fit history and archeology?" Some have tried to prove that the Bible's books are to be dated much later than what they claim to be. If these claims were proven to be true, then much of the accuracy of the Bible, especially in the case of the New Testament, can come into question and the prophecies, especially of the Old Testament, can be said to be written after the fact thus taking God out of them. Even though many times the New Testament is often the only part of the Bible considered, we will start with the Old Testament.

> "how can we be sure that the Bible we have today is what was originally written and not edited at a later date to fit history and archeology?"

With the Old Testament, there are not as many ancient (ancient meaning close to the original time written) manuscript copies of the Old Testament. There is a valid reason for this. The Hebrews, in dealing with their Scriptures (the Old Testament), held them with high regard since they contained the name of God, so they copied them with every detail being kept. If a manuscript were damaged or decaying, they would ceremonially bury the old copy while keeping the new one, sometimes considering the new one more valuable than the original. Some of the oldest manuscripts of the Old Testament are as follows: the Aleppo Codex dating back to the tenth century A.D. (originally the entire Hebrew Bible); the Leningrad Codex dating back to 1010 A.D. is the entire Old Testament; the Cairo Codex containing the former and latter prophets dating back to 895 A.D.; the Leningrad Codex of the Prophets written in 916 A.D. containing several of the books of the prophets; and the British Library Codex of the Pentateuch dating back to somewhere in the ninth or tenth century A.D. containing much of the Pentateuch. It is worth noting that the first two of these are from the Massoretic Text. A burnt scroll was found, and new methods were used to be able to read the scroll. It turns out the scroll has part of the Pentateuch (the first five books of the Bible and actually dates back to around 300 A.D., farther back than any other manuscripts with the exception of the Dead Sea Scrolls (to be looked at soon).

The Massoretes were scribes who were dedicated to keeping the Hebrew Scriptures in their original form, without any textual changes. They date back to about 500 A.D. continuing into the next four or five successive centuries. They are the ones who added vowel markings to the original text (the Hebrew text originally only contained consonants). These vowel markings were to tell how the words were to be pronounced. They do not however in any way change the text as written. The Massoretes also spent much time in counting the letters of each book, often noting the middle word and/or letter of a book of the Old Testament. In doing this they had the ability to make sure that what they had written was exactly a copy of the original they had. The Hebrew copy of the Old Testament is often called the Massoretic Text.

**Importance of Dead Sea Scrolls**

Some may still be alarmed at the time between when the originals were written and the date of these copies, hence the importance of the Dead Sea Scrolls. There may not be any Biblical archaeological find any more famous than that of the discovery of the Dead Sea Scrolls. About 200 of the scrolls discovered (many of which are fragments) contain parts of the Old Testament. The great Isaiah Scroll dates back to the first century B.C. and is really an updated version of the Massoretic Text, very close to our present Old Testament. Some parts of the scrolls show more of a liking to the Septuagint (the main Greek translation of the Old Testament dating back to 300-200 B.C.) and/or the Samaritan Pentateuch, an early form of the Hebrew text of the Pentateuch, the first five books of the Bible, (these two are evidences of the authenticity of the text that we have today) over the Massoretic Text. While there are some differences between the scrolls and the Massoretic Text, the differences are small, sometimes just spellings or word variations in translations. As Neil Lightfoot writes, *"The Biblical documents of the Dead Sea Scrolls are nothing short of sensational. The two Isaiah scrolls and many others as well, even though they go back as far as the B.C. era, demonstrate that the Old Testament was well preserved and accurately handed down to us."* Also J. Weingreen

*continued on page 49*

ARTIFACT GALLERY | 33

TOP LEFT: *Ancient mound of Jericho*
BOTTOM LEFT: *Tel El Armana tablets from 14 century BC confirm Egyptian and Babylonian captivity, that the Canaanites and the Hebrews had been enemies, confirmed the name of Jerusalem among other details from the book of Judges.*
RIGHT: *Ancient pool of Bethesda from John 5:2*

*Palace ruins in ancient city of Ebla, Syria where Ebla Tablets were discovered in 1974-75. 2500-2250 BC, Tablets validate the existence of the five cities mentioned in Genesis 14.*

## 34 | ARTIFACT GALLERY

LEFT: Moabite Stone, 840 BC, Text mentions Mesha, a king of Moab referenced in 2 Kings 3 as well as Yahweh. Discovered in Dhiban, Jordan, 1868. Louvre Museum. Image courtesy of wikipedia.com/Mzbt

RIGHT: Hebrew inscription on stone tablet. 1st Century BC, Speaks of a Messiah who will rise from the dead after three days.

Moabite Stone, Detail of lines 12-16, reconstructed from squeeze made before stone was broken in local dispute over ownership. Middle line reads "Take Nabau against Isreal". Image courtesy of wikipedia.com/Mzbt

Ancient Tablets | 35

*Tel Dan Stele, 870-750 BC, First reference to the name of David outside of Hebrew Bible. Also validates 2 Kings 8:28-29 telling of Hazael's victory at Ramoth-Gilead. Discovered in 1993-1994 during excavations in northern Isreal. Israel Museum, Jerusalem. Image courtesy of Wikipedia/OrenRozen*

*The Israelite Wall and Gate in Tel Dan built by King Jeroboam. Image courtesy of Gary Littwin*

## 36 | ARTIFACT GALLERY

Black Obelisk of Shalmaneser, 854-824 BC, Found in 1846 during excavation of the ancient Assyrian capital of Kalhu (Nimrud). These scenes show Jehu, king of Isreal bowing down to Assyrian king Shalmanser III both of which are recorded in I Kings 19, 2 Kings 9 and 2 Kings 10. British Museum.

Ancient Tablets | 37

LEFT: *Taylor Prism, 691 BC, Discovered in Nineveh, the ancient capital of the Assyrian Empire, in 1830. Annals of King Sennacherib describing the seige of Jerusalem during the reign of king Hezekiah. See 2 Kings 19, 2 Chronicles 32 and Isaiah 37. British Museum. Image courtesy of wikipedia.com/DavidCasto*
RIGHT: *Taylor Prism. Alternate view. Image courtesy of wikipedia.com/Hanay*

*Cyrus Cylinder, 6th Century BC, discovered in the ruins of Babylon in 1879. Inscription documents Cyrus allowing the Babylonian captives to return to their homeland as also recorded in Ezra 1. British Museum. Image courtesy of wikipedia.com/Prioryman*

## 38 | ARTIFACT GALLERY

*Dead Sea Scrolls, AD 30-50, Fragments on leather from the Book of Psalms. The Dead Sea Scrolls include 225 biblical texts from every book of the Old Testament except Esther. They were discovered in a series of twelve caves around the site known as Wadi Qumran near the Dead Sea in the West Bank (of the Jordan River) between 1946 and 1956 by Bedouin shepherds and a team of archeologists.*

Ancient Scrolls | 39

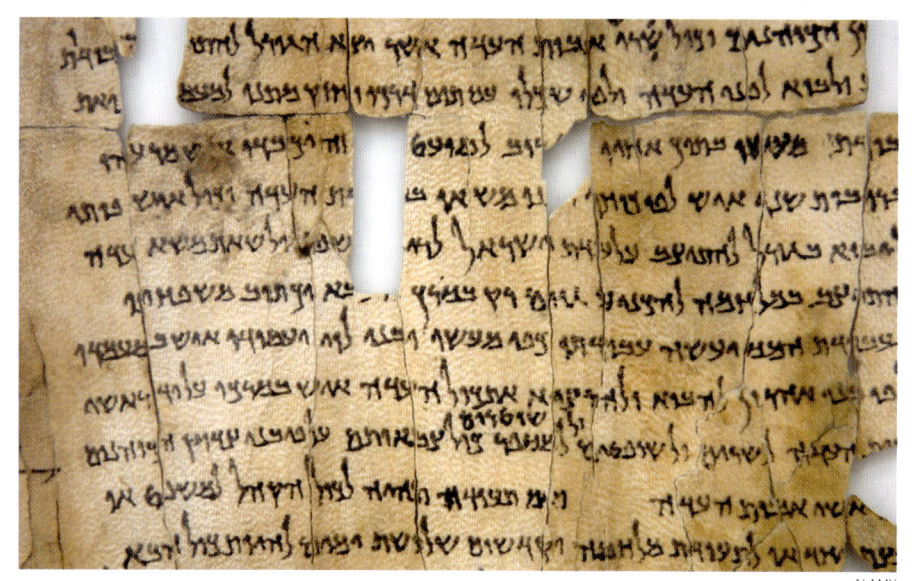

*Detail of Dead Sea Scrolls, 356-103 BC, The Isaiah Scroll is the best preserved of the biblical scrolls found in the Qumran caves. It is written in Hebrew and contains the entire Book of Isaiah. Written on 17 sheets of parchment, it is 24 feet long and 11 inches high. National Archeological Museum, Amman, Jordan.*

*Cave 4 where 75% of Dead Sea Scrolls were found in 1952.*

# Simplified Timeline of Biblical History
## 2000 BC – AD 2000

*Biblical characters shown in red. All times approximate

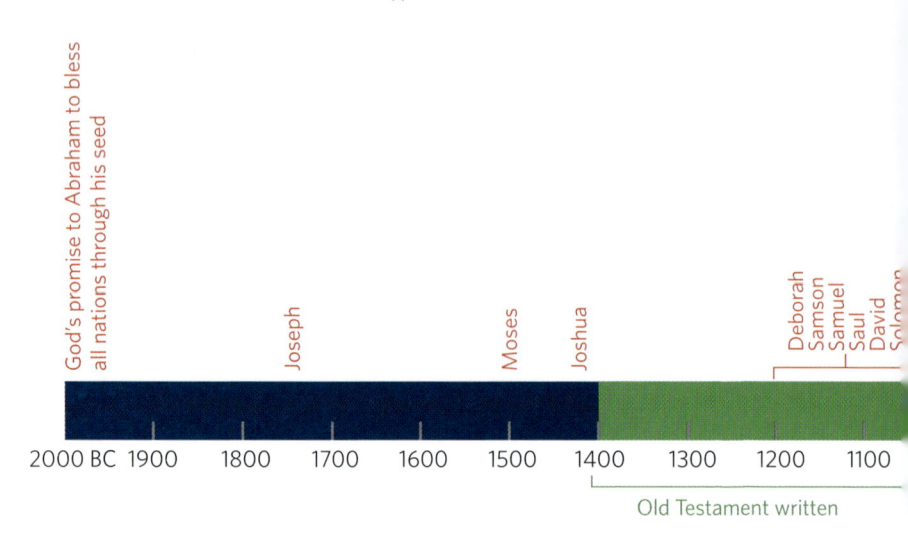

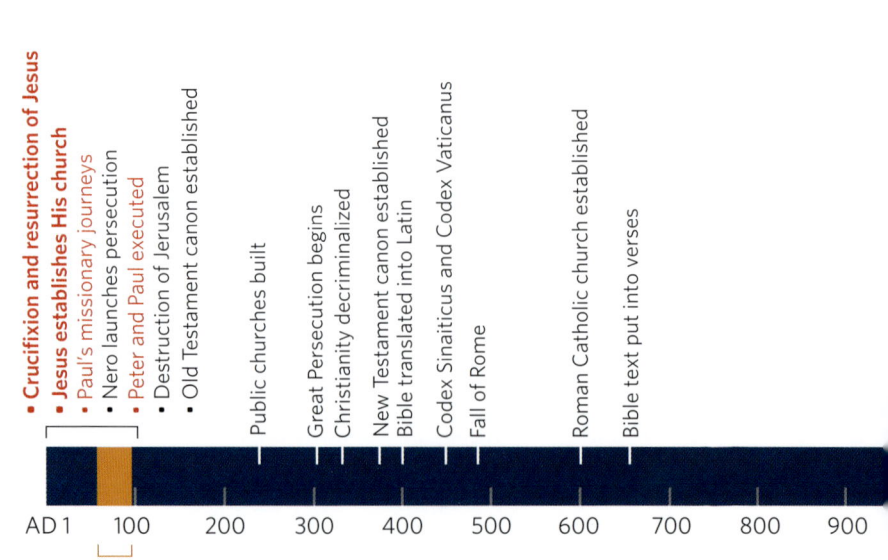

- God's promise to Abraham to bless all nations through his seed
- Joseph
- Moses
- Joshua
- Deborah
- Samson
- Samuel
- Saul
- David
- Solomon

2000 BC | 1900 | 1800 | 1700 | 1600 | 1500 | 1400 | 1300 | 1200 | 1100

Old Testament written

- Crucifixion and resurrection of Jesus
- Jesus establishes His church
- Paul's missionary journeys
- Nero launches persecution
- Peter and Paul executed
- Destruction of Jerusalem
- Old Testament canon established
- Public churches built
- Great Persecution begins
- Christianity decriminalized
- New Testament canon established
- Bible translated into Latin
- Codex Sinaiticus and Codex Vaticanus
- Fall of Rome
- Roman Catholic church established
- Bible text put into verses

AD 1 | 100 | 200 | 300 | 400 | 500 | 600 | 700 | 800 | 900

New Testament written

Timeline | 41

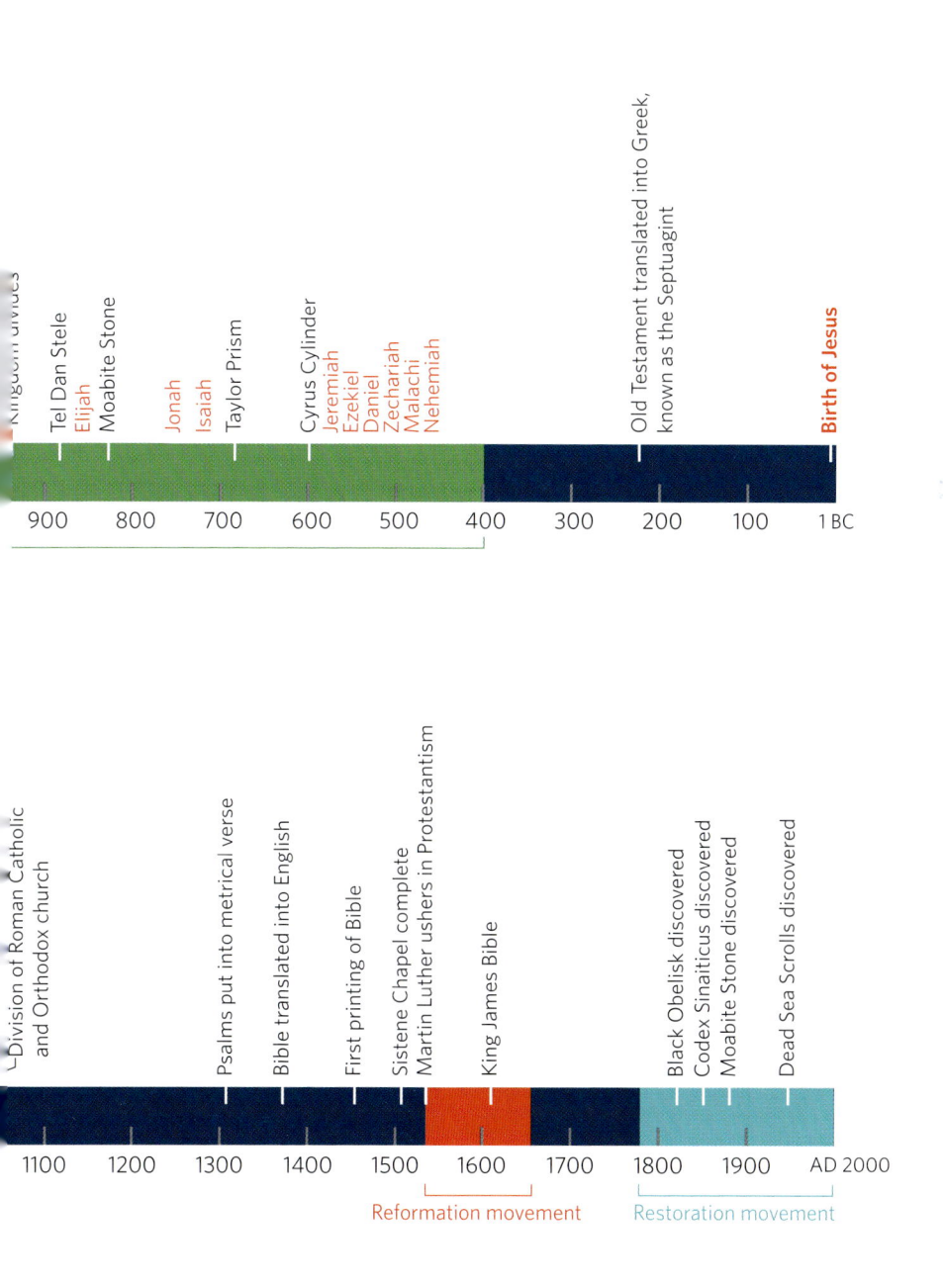

## BC Timeline (900 – 1 BC)

- Tel Dan Stele
- Elijah
- Moabite Stone
- Jonah
- Isaiah
- Taylor Prism
- Cyrus Cylinder
- Jeremiah
- Ezekiel
- Daniel
- Zechariah
- Malachi
- Nehemiah
- Old Testament translated into Greek, known as the Septuagint
- **Birth of Jesus**

## AD Timeline (1100 – AD 2000)

- Division of Roman Catholic and Orthodox church
- Psalms put into metrical verse
- Bible translated into English
- First printing of Bible
- Sistene Chapel complete
- Martin Luther ushers in Protestantism
- King James Bible
- Black Obelisk discovered
- Codex Sinaiticus discovered
- Moabite Stone discovered
- Dead Sea Scrolls discovered

Reformation movement

Restoration movement

42 | ARTIFACT GALLERY

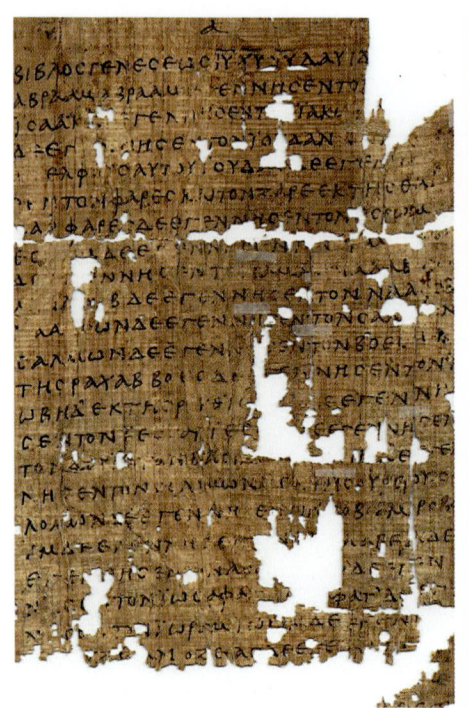

Oxyrhynchus Papyri and photographs from archeological site. Collection includes twenty-seven manuscripts that include part of the New Testament. 3rd century BC-3rd century AD. Image courtesy of papyrology.ox.ac.uk

LEFT: Papyrus 66, Bodmer Papyri collection, AD 200, Near complete codex of the Gospel of John. Found in Egypt in 1952. Currently housed at the Cologny-Geneva, Switzerland: Bibliotheca Bodmeriana.
RIGHT: Papyrus 4, late 2nd-early 3rd century Greek fragments of the Gospel of Luke. Currently housed in the Bibliothèque nationale de France.

## Papyri

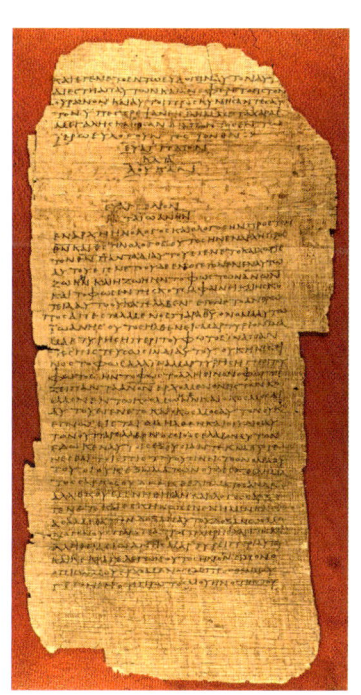

LEFT: *Papyrus 46, contains most of the Pauline epistles, one of the oldest extant New Testament manuscripts in Greek. Dated to AD 175-225. Shown is 2 Corinthians 11:33-12:9. University of Michigan Papyrus Collection.*
RIGHT: *Papyrus 75, containing nearly half of the books of Luke and John. Dated to AD 75-225. Vatican Library, Rome.*

*Chester Beatty texts, AD 200-400, Greek texts of the Old and New Testament on papyri. Found on the banks of the Nile, Egypt in 1920. Chester Beatty Library, Dublin.*

## 44 | ARTIFACT GALLERY

*Codex Vaticanus, 4th century, Uncial letters on vellum, Luke chapter 24 and John chapter 1. Listed in Vatican library's earliest catalog, 1475.*

LEFT: *Cover of Cairo Codex, Written in AD 827, Jerusalem. Hebrew text of minor and major Prophet books. Hebrew University, Jerusalem.*
RIGHT: *Cover of Leningrad Codex, AD 1008, Cairo. Complete manuscript of Old Testament in Hebrew. National Library of Russia.*

*Codex Alexandrinus, 5th Century Greek manuscript of Bible. Shown here is the end of the 2 Epistle of Peter and the beginning of the 1 Epistle of John in the same column. British Library, London.*

## 46 | ARTIFACT GALLERY

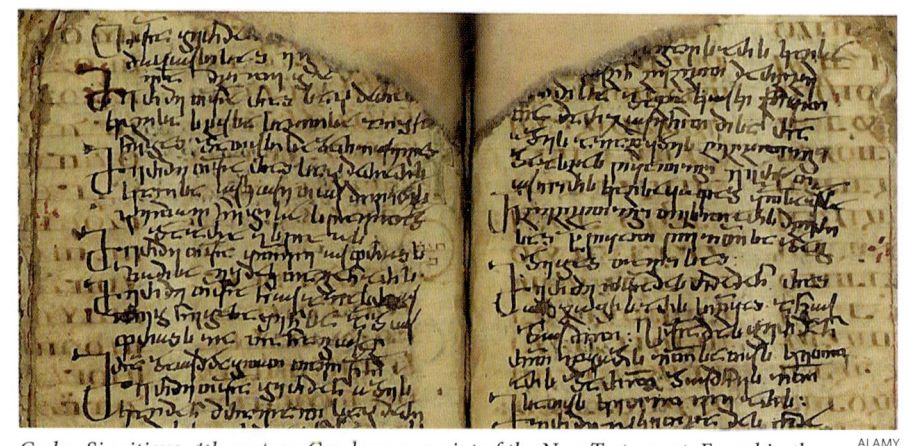

*Codex Sinaiticus, 4th century Greek manuscript of the New Testament. Found in the monastery of St. Catherine in the 19th century. On display at Mt. Sinai, Egypt*

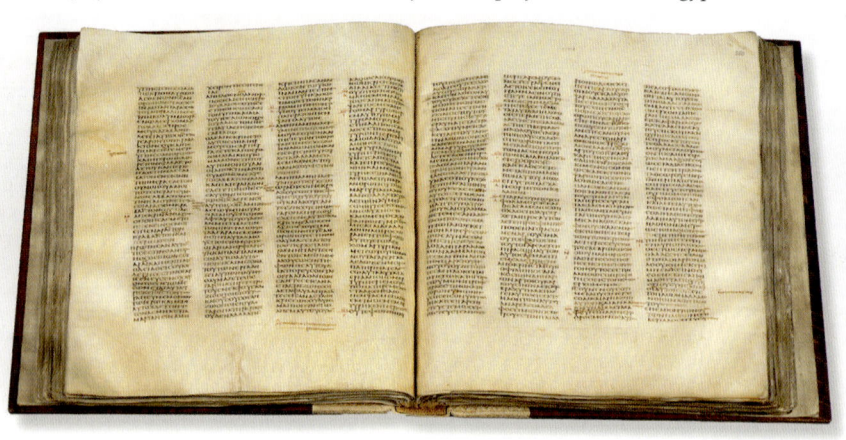

*Codex Sinaiticus, British Library portion.*

*Muratorian Fragment. 7th Century copy of a Greek text written around AD 170. Includes list of most of the books of the New Testament. Bibliotheca Ambrosiana, Milan.*

The Didache, also known as The Teaching of the Twelve Apostles. A brief anonymous
early Christian treatise, dated by most scholars to the first century.

*Aleppo Codex, AD 930, Northern Isreal, Earliest manuscript of complete Hebrew bible. Excerpt from Book of Psalms. Isreal Museum.*

*Aleppo Codex, Excerpt from Joshua 1:1. Image courtesy of Aleppocodex.org*

writes, "It should therefore be stated explicitly that, when we survey the Hebrew Bible as a whole, the incidence of copyists' errors is statistically very few indeed. Even allowing for the intrusion of occasional errors in the received Hebrew text, it is remarkable how faithfully it was transmitted." To sum up how good these manuscripts are to the original text, here is an ancient excerpt telling how detail oriented the Jewish scribes were in copying the Old Testament (in this case with the Pentateuch):

"A synagogue scroll must be written on the skins of clean animals, prepared for the particular use of the synagogue by a Jew. ...The length of each column must not extend over less than forty-eight, or more than sixty lines. ...The ink should be black, neither red, green, nor any other colour and be prepared according to a definite recipe. An authentic copy must be exemplar, from which the transcriber ought not in the least to deviate. No word or letter, not even an yod, must be written from memory, the scribe not having looked at the codex before him.... Besides this, the copyist must sit in full Jewish dress, wash his whole body, not begin to write the name of God with a pen newly dipped in ink, ... ."

## New Testament Manuscripts far outnumber other manuscripts

Now let's turn our attention to the New Testament. Even though it is dissected much more than the Old Testament, there are even more manuscripts and evidences to its authenticity than to the Old Testament. To start with, let's just compare it to other early works. Homer's epics, the Iliad and Odyssey, date back to the time somewhere between the eighth century B.C. (or earlier) and the seventh century B.C.. Our earliest copy of Homer's works dates to the third century B.C., centuries after their composition. There are over 1,000 copies or partial copies of Homer's works. The New Testament has about 20,000 lines in Greek, while the Iliad has about 15,600 lines. Only forty lines (about 400 words) of the New Testament are questioned, but 764 lines of the Iliad are questioned (5% compared to .5%). For the Indian epic of Mahabharata, roughly eight times bigger than the Iliad and Odyssey when combined, about 10% of it is questioned. Of

Caesar's writings from between 100 BC and 44 BC, the earliest copy is 900 A.D. and there are only manuscript copies. There are many other works from that time period to compare to the New Testament, but it is much the same or worse in comparison; that is there are more manuscript witnesses and less time differential for the New Testament than for the other works.

Here are a couple of quotes to summarize what we have seen:

"...since scholars accept as generally trustworthy the writings of the ancient classics even though the earliest MSS were written so long after the original writings and the number of extant MSS is in many instances so small, it is clear that the reliability of the text of the N.T. is likewise assured." - J. Harold Greenlee

"There is no body of ancient literature in the world which enjoys such a wealth of good textual attestation as the New Testament."- F. F. Bruce

So what about some of these 5300 manuscripts that are copies of part or all of the New Testament? Here are some of the most important. The Vatican Manuscript dates back to the fourth century and contains most of the Old and New Testaments in Greek. The Sinaitic Manuscript, also from the fourth century, contains most of the Old Testament and all of the New Testament (in fact the oldest complete copy of the New Testament). The Alexandrian Manuscript contains most of the Old Testament and a good portion of the New Testament (plus a couple of books of the Apocrypha added because of the region it was from) dating back to the fifth century. There are also the papyri such as: The Oxyrhynchus Papyri which includes twenty-seven manuscripts with parts of the New Testament dating back to the second, third, and early fourth centuries (all older than the three given above); the Chester Beatty Papyri consisting of eleven manuscripts containing portions of the Old Testament (in Greek) and portions of the New Testament; and the Bodmer Papyri consisting of parts of the two testaments in Greek and in Coptic (Egyptian) some dating back to around 200 A.D. and into the early part of the third century.

> *"There is no body of ancient literature in the world which enjoys such a wealth of good textual attestation as the New Testament."* - F. F. BRUCE

Other important papyri are: P4, P64, and P67 which contain parts of Matthew and Luke and date back to late second century; P46 which contains a good portion of Paul's letters and dates back to the early part of the third century; P52 (the John Rylands Fragment) which contains a small portion of John (the fragment is very small itself) and dates back to the first half of the second century (putting to death the idea of a very late date of authorship of John); P66 (part of the Bodmer Papyri) has an extensive part of John and dates to around 200 A.D.; and P75 (another part of the Bodmer Papyri) which contains large portions of Luke and John and dates back to between 175 and 225 A.D..

This evidence of the manuscripts is well summarized by Sir Frederick Kenyon:

*"One word or warning already referred to, must be emphasized in conclusion. No fundamental doctrine of the Christian faith rests on a disputed reading…It cannot be too strongly asserted that in substance the text of the Bible is certain: Especially is this the case with the New Testament. The number of manuscripts of the New Testament, of early translations from it, and of quotations from it in the oldest writers of the Church, is so large that it is practically certain that the true reading of every doubtful passage is preserved in some one or other of these ancient authorities. This can be said of no other ancient book in the world."*

His last statement is very telling and is not just a wish. It is a fact!

## Outside writings give evidence to Biblical content

Now let's look at writings outside of the Bible that give evidence to what is in the Bible. Three writings from around 100 A.D. known as the Epistle of Barnabas, the Didache, and Clement's letter to the church in Corinth all quote from the New Testament books, including Matthew, Mark, and Luke, Acts, Romans, 1 Corinthians, Ephesians, Titus, Hebrews, 1 Peter, and possibly from some others. Ignatius, who wrote around the beginning of the second century, quoted from Matthew, John, Romans, 1 and 2 Corinthians, Galatians, Ephesians, Philippians, 1 and 2 Timothy, Titus, and with possible references to Mark, Luke, Acts, Colossians, 2 Thessalonians, Philemon, Hebrews, and 1 Peter. Polycarp wrote to the Philippian church around 120 A.D. and quoted from the Gospels, Acts, Romans, 1 and 2 Corinthians, Galatians, Ephesians, Philippians, 2 Thessalonians, 1 and 2 Timothy, Hebrews, 1 Peter, and 1 John.

These are a few of who are known as the Apostolic Fathers; they were Christians who lived in that period directly after the apostles (maybe even overlapping in time). Besides these mostly mainstream writers, there were also the Gnostics, a heretical sect, who also quoted from the books of the New Testament as early as the middle of the second century. There are other Christian writers dating back to the third century and the fourth centuries who also are given the general title "church fathers"; these also quote the books of the New Testament. Thus, we have the following conclusion George W. Dehoff:

We conclude that the New Testament if lost could be restored from the writings of the "church fathers" in any century back to the first one; that the New Testament as we now have it has existed and been accepted as genuine and authentic in every century since the apostles lived.

**First century historians validate the Bible**

In addition to the Christians who quoted from the Bible, there are non-Christians who validate the Bible with their writings. Josephus, a Jewish historian from the first century, refers to John the Baptist, the Pharisees, the Sadducees, the Herodians, the death of Herod (it is similar to Luke 12), Felix, Drusilla, and Bernice, all in the New Testament. He also has a very famous passage mentioning Jesus:

Now there was, about this time, Jesus, a wise man, if it be lawful to call him a man; for He performed many wonderful works. He was a teacher of such men as received the truth with pleasure. He drew over to him many of the Jews and also the Gentiles. This was the Christ. And when Pilate, at the instigation of the principal men among us, had condemned him to the cross, those who had loved him from the first did not cease to adhere to him. For He appeared to them alive the third day, the divine prophets having foretold these and ten thousand other wonderful things concerning him. And the title of Christians so named for him subsists to this day.

Some say that part of this writing was inserted later by Christians. Even if that were true, the part of the passage held to be authentic would still back up the fact that Jesus was a real man. There was also Tacitus who lived in the first century; he also mentions that Christianity came from Jesus, a man killed by Pilate, and that the Christians were tortured and killed by the Romans. Likewise, Suetonius, Pliny, Hegesippus, Lucian, edicts of Roman emperors, Porphyry, Celsus, and Julian all from between the first and early fourth centuries wrote commenting about Christ, Christians, New Testament books, and even verses from the New Testament.

**Objections to the inspiration of the Bible**

Some have argued that even though these New Testament books date back to the first century and are not dated to a later time period as doubters have argued, the books of the New Testament were not really inspired since they were not canonized until 393 A.D. and 397 A.D. in North Africa. While these dates are times when groups of men of the Church declared what was inspired and what was not, it does not imply that these men really decided what was inspired and what was not. In 140 A.D. there was a man named Marcion who had his own list of accepted books; this list is not the same as our New Testament, but Marcion was a heretic because he believed that the God of the Old Testament was inferior to the God of the New Testament. Thus he believed that any book with Old Testament connections should be discarded. We see that he wrote down his list out of bias. There is also the Muratorian Fragment that dates back to the end of the second century. It lists as accepted books 22 of the 27 New

Testament books, plus a few extra. There are other references early on to accepted books, but in reality there are only a few of the New Testament books which were even questioned by Christians by the middle of the second century: Hebrews, 2 Peter, 2 and 3 John, James, Jude, the Epistle of Barnabas, the Shepherd of Hermas, the Didache, and the Gospel according to the Hebrews. In 367 A.D. Athanasius lists the 27 books of the New Testament, and others followed afterward with the same list. While all this may still seem troublesome to some, we have to remember first of all that at that time there was no internet, no cars, no phones, no planes, no fax machines, no trains, and even no printing press, so for letters or books that were already accepted in parts of the world it would take time to be accepted or even get to other parts of the world, even though the known world was smaller back then. Likewise if some writings were accepted mistakenly for short periods of time in some parts of the world, it would take time, too, for these to be discovered not to be inspired. F. F. Bruce states it this way:

One thing must be emphatically stated. The New Testament books did not become authoritative for the Church because they were formally included in a canonical list; on the contrary, the Church included them in her canon because she already regarded them as divinely inspired, recognizing their innate worth and generally apostolic authority, direct or indirect.

**Is the Bible full of errors?**

The last objection to the inspiration of the Bible that many make is that the Bible is full of errors and contradictions. You may find several of these in "Bible Errors and Contradictions" by P. Wesley Edwards. First let us deal with the one Mr. Edwards starts with: Genesis 32:30 where Jacob says that he has seen God face to face and lived versus John 1:18 that says no one has seen God at any time. To say that these are in conflict with each other is to completely take the Genesis verse out of context. This is Jacob talking after he has wrestled with a man from God, oftentimes considered an angel by many. This man could be the Word, A.K.A. Jesus, and maybe that is why he said what he said about seeing God, or it is an angel representing God there to bless

> "We conclude that the New Testament if lost could be restored from the writings of the "church fathers" in any century back to the first one; that the New Testament as we now have it has existed and been accepted as genuine and authentic in every century since the apostles lived." - GEORGE W. DEHOFF

Jacob after the wrestling match. Either way Jacob's pronouncement of seeing God is not literal when put in the context of God the Father and does not contradict what John says in 1:18. Next is Matthew 19:26 saying God can do anything versus Judges 1:19 which Mr. Edwards interprets as saying that technology, iron chariots, defeated the tribe of Judah backed by God. First of all the "he" in the translation refers to the tribe of Judah (a "collective" pronoun in English); some translations even translate it as "they". Also the Judges' verse is in a collection of verses that have several tribes that do not win their lands at that point in time; Judges 2:1-5 says that they did not obey God so God did not give them all of the lands that He had wanted to give them which goes along perfectly with an early Jewish interpretation or paraphrase. We then see Mark 15:25 which says the crucifixion was at the third hour, but John 19:14-16 says the events leading up to it were about the sixth hour. When taking into account that Mark could be writing according to Jewish time and John according to Roman time, then the times do not conflict at all, but actually agree. One more example: 2 Kings 24:8 (saying that Jehoiachin was eight years old when he became king while 2 Chronicles 36:9 says that he was eighteen. Jehoiachin was crowned by his father at age eight, but he did not reign until he was eighteen after his father died). We could continue on, but time keeps us from answering every single alleged contradiction; we see from these few examples what is usually the case, either the problem arises from taking a verse out of context or from the lack of taking time to delve into the background of the verse(s). Sometimes it is just a matter of taking time to think of the possibilities. There is always an answer.

What about just some of the Bible being inspired because we have not dealt with every verse of every chapter of every book? First let's look at why someone would look at the Bible this way. If we were to delve deep enough we would find that that person probably does not want to believe in all of the Bible because some part does not coincide with what he/she believes or practices or lives. In other words, they have made themselves the authority because they do not want to give up a part of their lifestyle. This type of thinking goes against everything we have just looked at. It eventually says that man knows more than God, which of course is false. In most cases it also can be shown that most of the people who now say only parts of the Bible are inspired were originally convinced to become Christians because of the entire Bible, not just part. It is only afterward that they decide not to accept everything in the Bible because, again, of their lifestyle. If the main reason someone does not accept the Bible as inspired is because it does not say what he/she believes it should say, then that person is really putting himself/herself in the position of God - one who decides what is right or wrong. Is man really that smart?

In conclusion, we have dealt with different areas of question about the Bible being accurate, and being the word of God. We have briefly, very briefly, looked at the Bible in regards to science, history and archeology, its origins, and its validity. In all of these areas, when one really takes the time to do a careful search, the Bible comes out as authoritatively the word of God. The problem we have as human beings is sometimes distinguishing between what man believes, Christians and non-Christians alike, and what the facts and the Bible really say.

> "I believe that the next half century will determine if we will advance the cause of Christian civilization or revert to the horrors of brutal paganism."
>
> -THEODORE ROOSEVELT

CHAPTER 3

# Is Jesus For Real?

### BY STEVE CANTRELL

WE'VE NOW GIVEN THOROUGH CONSIDERATION to two of the fundamental questions every human needs to consider: whether God actually exists, and whether the Bible is valid as a communication from him and can still be trusted today. In light of the things you hear constantly these days implying that these are disproven ideas, you may have been surprised that the logic and evidence are so insurmountable for both. In fact, any person who diligently and honestly seeks and considers all the available evidence comes away convinced beyond doubt. But so what? What difference does it make in real life?

## The Jewish carpenter - God in human flesh

The answer to that, of course, is in the central figure of the Bible: a Jewish carpenter and noted teacher named Jesus, a man who claimed to be the "son of God" and in fact God in human flesh. If Jesus is for real, we need to know it, for if he is who he claimed to be then his words are the words of God and his teachings and promises and commandments are the most important thing we'll ever encounter. Not surprisingly, he is the most influential figure in human history, and the founders of this nation not only name his commandments unabashedly as the foundation of our laws and government but stated that such a foundation is what made it a great nation for people of any other belief as well. Jesus even made the outrageous claim that no one could come to God the Father except through him! On the other hand, if he's not God's messenger and son, we can very confidently ignore everything he ever said and simply choose the way that seems right to us. Would you agree that this might turn out to be the central question of our lives?

If we're going to continue on this journey of discovery, scrutinizing evidence and considering it logically and fairly, how shall we find the answer to this momentous question? Shrugging it off or pretending we can't know the answer certainly won't do, and we can't afford to make a wrong assumption and ignore him. (Conversely, some might say that it's safer just to believe him whether he's real or not since that would be a "safe" mistake if there's no life after this one. That doesn't seem like much of a basis for devoting your life to a person and cause that might be a fake.) Neither would we serve the reader very well by simply saying that Jesus is real because the Bible says so. Sure, we've examined solid evidence that the Bible is verified and corroborated like no other work in history, but we need to look beyond that too.

> ...God never asks us to throw intelligent reason out the window.

If there is independent reasoning and evidence for the validity of both the Bible and Jesus, then they further confirm each other nicely and with full consistency (as it should be), but they can't just depend on each other for confirmation in a worthless circular-reasoning fashion. And if either can be shown false then the other becomes highly suspect as well if not an outright fabrication. So we would hope to find evidence either confirming or refuting the identity and claims of Jesus not only in the Bible but in independent sources as well. As we seek the answer, we should be honest and open enough to follow the evidence wherever it leads us, and we ought to have our brains fully engaged. Some believers say that we should simply accept his deity by faith and not look at logic and evidence to support it, but God never asks us to throw intelligent reason out the window. Instead we find a rock-solid foundation for faith in what has already been shown to us by incontrovertible evidence throughout human history. Faith involves believing certain things we haven't seen yet based upon that confident foundation, but definitely not things that are completely incompatible with logic and known fact. Fortunately, as we begin an inquest into the true identity of Jesus, we will see that the answers lie before us and are ready for scrutiny.

**Jesus - Lord, liar or lunatic?**

Perhaps a logical place to start is in defining the possible conclusions about who Jesus was, and then proceeding to consider the evidence and logic for and against each one. It used to be popular to claim that Jesus never existed at all and is purely a myth. No one even tries to say that anymore because his life and his impact on history are known beyond doubt from so many different reputable and independently confirming sources. One might be far more credible in claiming that Abraham Lincoln never actually existed. Dismissing that idea, probably the best known logical construct for this quest is the "trilemma" (a critical and usually difficult choice between three options, at least some of which if not all are mutually exclusive) which noted author C. S. Lewis adapted from the nineteenth century Scottish preacher John Duncan. The basic choices for Jesus are often stated as Lord, Liar, or Lunatic. That is, in claiming to be God and the human incarnation of God, Jesus must be the Lord as he claims, or a delusional lunatic, or the filthiest sort of liar and blasphemer. We might add a fourth possibility since many now choose to believe that he is merely a legend, a noted and wise teacher and a good man who never claimed to be divine but was eventually elevated to that status by the embellished folklore of many generations. All of these are worthy of consideration.

One of these possibilities is readily and properly dismissed. Any mere human who actually believes himself to be God is more likely to be an uncontrolled psychotic instead. That doesn't include everyone who claims to be God or his special prophet or other such equivalent. There have been plenty of those throughout history who aren't crazy, just wicked and perhaps cunningly so. But any mortal man who actually believes such a thing about himself is as delusional as can be, and without fail everyone around him becomes aware of his mental status within minutes. These are not the people who leave profound moral and religious teachings that captivate the world and endure through thousands of years, gaining untold millions of followers. The accounts of Jesus in secular history show us a man who was a most remarkable and influential teacher in his own day, to the amazement of scholars and fishermen alike. This is not the picture of a madman. It's worth noting that in our own modern day, even those who do not accept his claims of being heaven's messenger regard him as a masterful teacher whose mark endures through the ages. That's no lunatic.

**The legend argument**

What of the legend argument? This may be the most common conclusion we encounter these days. The idea is viable enough: A good and contemplative man grows up in a small town, without much education but with the kind of wisdom you don't learn in school. He sees through the hypocrisy and distorted teaching which the religious authorities of his day are imposing on the people and he has the conviction and guts to call their bluff and start teaching a better and truer way. He gains a following. His popularity continues to grow even in the generations after his death, and as the stories are repeated verbally from one generation to the next he begins to take on a much larger life than the one he actually lived. His story is adjusted to make it match some ancient prophecies, some miraculous deeds are fabricated to really dress it up, and finally he emerges as something he never claimed at all: the Son of God! And if this is what he is, a legend born of wishful thinking, then we may surely and safely ignore him altogether or at best include him with Socrates and Plato and some of history's more influential thinkers, giving him a nod of appreciation and respect but finding no promise or authority in him and certainly feeling no obligation to follow commandments that surely he never actually delivered anyway. This is such a comfortable and "nice" way to evade any real thought about Jesus and any need to confidently know the truth about him.

> The consistent accounts of the gospel writers are also consistent with what was written by secular, government-commissioned historians of the day.

That easy way out evaporates when we see that the legend idea just doesn't fit with the known facts. Legends take time to develop, a few hundred years and multiple generations at the very least. They also develop verbally (ever play an old game called "telephone" or "gossip"?) since written historical records preclude the gradual changing and embellishment that give rise to folklore and legends. Finally, legends only grow in the absence of witnesses who know the real facts and can correct the record. In the case of Jesus, all of these things fail completely. Let's take the timing first. You may have heard that the gospel accounts (Matthew, Mark, Luke, John) which provide the greatest detail about Jesus along with several other New Testament accounts, were written down around 150 to 200 or even more years after his death, giving just enough time for exaggeration and embellishment to occur, and have been further adapted through the centuries to enrich the fantasy. Nothing could be further from the truth. Because of the dedicated and meticulous efforts of so many scholars who have gone before us, we have known for centuries that the gospel accounts not only were written down but were carefully copied and widely distributed shortly after AD 100. This in itself is such an early date as to wipe out possibility of any significant embellishment, especially when the various accounts are consistent and so overlapping in their details. This date has been pushed back numerous times as archaeologists continue to discover even earlier collections of manuscripts. (In every case and regardless of where found, the content matches to an incredible degree of accuracy.)

It now seems that Mark's account was committed to papyrus around AD 60 if not earlier. As this chapter is being written in late 2016, the recent discovery of an accurately reproduced fragment of Mark glued into an Egyptian burial mask dated around 70 - 80 AD is just the latest confirmation, showing that this historical account of Jesus was spread far and wide within thirty or forty years of his death and maybe even earlier than that. The other gospel accounts have similar very early dates now confidently ascribed to them. The weight of this evidence is clear, but there's even more to consider. The consistent accounts of the gospel writers are also consistent with what was written by secular, government-commissioned historians of the day. The works of Flavius Josephus are the best known examples. He was not a follower of Jesus and makes only brief mention which nevertheless notes the huge societal impact of Jesus during his lifetime. Consider further that these very early accounts were written in the presence of plenty of eyewitnesses to the events recorded, including any number of them who were hostile to Jesus and his followers. You don't write fictional accounts when most of the people who saw it all happen are still right there to set the record straight, and especially when plenty of those eyewitnesses would love nothing more than to be able to contradict the account if they could. The theory of Jesus-as-legend goes down in flames when we actually examine the facts. And just as covered so well in the previous chapter, the Bible manuscripts have been preserved through the ensuing millennia with a degree of accuracy unparalleled by any other work in world history. The error-checking methods used in their propagation are actually forerunners of the algorithms now used in the copying of digital computer files. Could the story of Jesus possibly be a product of legend and wishful thinking? No, unless one simply refuses to look at the evidence.

### Was Jesus a blasphemer?

We come then to a determination of original truthfulness, the most critical question. We must consider the possibility that Jesus was a deliberate liar and con artist, and necessarily his companion disciples along with him. Regardless of whether one is initially inclined to believe in Jesus or not, it's a question that needs to be considered and definitely not one to be taken lightly. After all, the horrible blasphemy of falsely claiming what can only belong to God was exactly the basis for his execution. He wouldn't be the first or the last to make a dishonest claim to divine status, either. First, we need to be clear that he really did claim such a status. There's no doubt about this. Time and space restraints make it impossible to recount all the references here, but the narrative accounts are bursting with the claims he made and the definitive ways he stated it. When the Jewish authorities put him on trial and hired witnesses to testify against him, this was in fact the only point they could get their witnesses to agree upon: he was a blasphemer, because he claimed to be God. And because they assumed that claim to be a vile falsehood, it became sufficient justification for the death penalty. He could have saved his skin by renouncing his claim to deity then and there. Instead he made the claim repeatedly and beyond any ambiguity, and he died for it. Was that death the sacrifice of the son of God, or the just punishment for a lie of gravest magnitude? Lewis correctly points out that there is no option in between. What will the evidence show, and what conclusion makes logical sense?

## Old Testament prophesies were always consistent

We should note again that there is a wealth of scholarly reference material looking at this question, and in the interest of making the chapter you're now looking at fairly short and quickly digestible we're making the briefest summary of many volumes of solid information. It is hoped that the reader may want to delve into some of the references cited at the end of the chapter among others. When you do, you'll be struck with the quality and volume of corroborating evidence. (Fair warning: when atheists undertake a serious investigation in order to discredit Christianity, most of them emerge from it as unshakably convinced believers instead. It's that complete and definitive.) To determine if Jesus was a liar and a fake, let's first think just briefly about the attributes of the Bible itself.

The Old Testament has a consistent and recurring message from start to finish, even though committed to "paper" by dozens of writers over several thousand years. Its prophecies and message all speak of a Messiah who will be coming to bring salvation. The writers of those times didn't know who it would be or how far in the future, but they recorded and preserved a unified message. How could you get people to go to that much trouble (and in some cases death) for nothing? How could you get them to write a consistent set of stories over all those centuries if it were all fabricated? Who could oversee such a grand conspiracy? Those questions come into even sharper focus when we move to the New Testament. Many of these writers actually spent several years of their lives traveling and working with Jesus, and others who came shortly after his death devoted the remainder of their lives to his cause. Would they do that for a liar and blaspheming fraud? They would have known very clearly if that's what he was. Why would Jesus give up his family and pleasant life to be a homeless preacher, suffering frequent ridicule and then torture and execution, just so he could perpetrate a lie upon us all? What's the incentive? How did he manage to engineer his life so as to be the only man in history who has fulfilled all the ancient prophecies foretold of the Messiah? (It's unfortunate that space doesn't allow reviewing all these things in detail here, but as for this question, the odds of it happening at random are far beyond astronomical.) Conspiracies take a lot of work to pull off, and they occur when people have an overwhelming and typically evil desire to bring about some end which usually involves amassing money or power for themselves. Think about it: the lie of Jesus as Messiah with all that it involves would be the most massive and frankly impossible conspiracy in human history. For what purpose? So virtually everyone involved could be ridiculed, impoverished, tortured, and executed?

    Let's delve a little further into that last thought for a moment. As we noted a moment ago, if Jesus were a liar there were a large number of people who would have known it and would have said so. We know that his earthly younger brothers were skeptics about his claims and mission early in his ministry. Yet later they became not only devoted believers but leaders in the church, and may have given their lives for his cause as well. Do you do that for someone you have reason to know is a liar and a fraud, or do you do that when you have seen convincing proof that Jesus is exactly who he claimed to be? The same story holds for the apostles who were his constant companions the last three years of his life. From both the New Testament and other historical accounts, we know that they spent the rest of their lives preaching his message and largely suffering for it, and of the majority of them whose fates we know, every one except John was executed for that faith. Amazingly, not a single one of them, even faced with violent death, ever finally admitted that the whole thing was a lie that Jesus had started and convinced them to carry on. If he were a liar and fraud these are the people who would have known it for sure, and every one of them would have "sung like a canary" to save their own lives and spare their families. The fact that they accepted death instead speaks volumes about who they knew him to be and how convincingly they knew it.

**Jesus proved He was God in human form**

Just how did they know? Further, how did the masses know? We have accounts that in those days, just like now, there were plenty of impostors who falsely claimed authority from God. We can surely say that Jesus stood in stark contrast to any others because of his message and because he sought no wealth or power. That's not the central reason, though. Then and now, it's important to use the good sense we're capable of. If someone claims to be the incarnate God, or his authorized prophet, must we be left to guess whether it's true or not? No. God has not left us to wonder, nor does he ask us to accept things that defy plain truth. He did something with Jesus just as with his chosen messengers through the ages before and in the few decades after Jesus. Their authority as God's designated speakers was made plain, beyond any honest doubt at all, by the display of signs and wonders which transcended natural law and could have come from no source except the very God who created those natural laws. Consistently, those whom we are asked to accept as representing God with divine revelation authority -- and above all, as God in human form with the name Jesus -- have been validated by miraculous confirmation. (You might note that such confirmation is noticeably absent from many in these latter days who claim to be specially ordained by God.)

Before we go any further, we must seriously consider whether miraculous events are even possible. Many people today will flatly deny that any miraculous thing could ever have occurred. We're told that it's impossible because it's contrary to science and we're just a little too intelligent for that kind of superstition these days. In essence, the argument is that I've never seen it, I can't measure it, I can't imagine it, it's contrary to the laws of nature, and therefore it has never happened. Even many people who believe in the existence of God and otherwise generally accept the Bible as valid will quietly say that they no longer believe any miraculous events literally occurred. "It's not scientific. It's just not possible." The problem with this approach is that it assumes the present person's human intelligence and experience to be the ultimate authority and the final arbiter of reality (while disregarding the carefully documented witness accounts of others) and in so doing it leads to an intentional and very arrogant ignorance. The fact that you refuse to consider something doesn't make its existence or validity any less. Imagine the analogy of a housefly stating very authoritatively that stories of a deadly contraption called a flyswatter are nothing but myth. After all, he might explain, he's never seen one or talked to another fly that has seen one, he can't measure or test one or conduct an experiment to disprove or verify its existence, and can't conceive of such a thing existing, so therefore it does not and cannot exist. He can continue with his arrogant denial of the possible existence of the flyswatter right up to the time he encounters one.

The key is actually in that very assessment that a miraculous event is not scientific and therefore has never occurred. It's contrary to the known laws of nature, and therefore it's just not possible. Not possible unless you happen to be the infinite God who created this universe with its laws of nature and can override them if you choose, none of which any human or any force of nature itself can do. That's the whole point. Events that are properly defined as miraculous are those which defy natural law and could not have occurred other than at the hand of God himself. It's not contrary to science per se; it's by very definition beyond science. That is precisely why the truly miraculous is the confirmation of God's action.

## No, miracles are not possible. Unless you're God, that is.

God has confirmed the identity of his true prophets throughout history in this way (which is necessarily accompanied by the absolute truthfulness of their message and the absolute accuracy of their prophecy). He didn't expect us to accept the word of any messenger we couldn't be sure about. And let's be sure to note that we're not talking about simple parlor tricks or sleight of hand. No, God's style runs more towards immediately healing a man who has been paralyzed from birth or one who has been blind all his life, things well known to the entire community and things that can't be faked or explained in any other way. John 11 is a classic example of the miraculous confirmation of the deity of Jesus. His beloved friend Lazarus dies, but Jesus intentionally waits until he has been in the grave and decomposing for nearly four days, then raises him from the dead. Some may say "People weren't as sophisticated back then, so they were probably easily fooled by a talented illusionist." That dismissal really doesn't work when a corpse is stone cold and stinks of four days of death. The hundreds and sometimes thousands of eyewitnesses of the miracles of Jesus weren't stupid. It's noteworthy that even his worst enemies couldn't deny his miracles and didn't try. The examples in Matthew 12 and Mark 3 illustrate their hatred of him coupled with the fact that they still could not deny the irrefutable miraculous power of God displayed in front of them. Presented with such a dilemma but determined to deny him, they were left only to claim that his miraculous power came from Satan. (In simple and brilliant logic with a dose of sarcasm, Jesus demolished their idiotic and self-defeating argument from several different angles at once.)

### Jesus' miracles proved who He was

The fact is, we see the identity of Jesus confirmed by miraculous power again and again. It is indeed a shame that this short discussion can't recount every documented instance recorded for us; the eyewitness accounts outnumber and outweigh the support of any other ancient literature and as noted they come from both his believers and his enemies alike. The secular historian Josephus notes them as a matter of fact. When Peter and the other apostles address the Pentecost crowd in Jerusalem as recorded in Acts 2, they make this point exactly. Speaking to much the same crowd that had called for and watched the execution of Jesus a few weeks earlier, Peter describes him as "Jesus of Nazareth, a man attested to you by God with mighty works and wonders and signs that God did through him in your midst, as you yourselves know." (Acts 2:22) How interesting that he observes that they already knew this to be true. Many in that crowd hated Jesus and were pleased with his death, and everyone there knew whether the words were true and would have shouted him down immediately if they weren't. Instead they came to the horrible conclusion that they had just murdered the very son of God, consistent with what Jesus himself had said: "If I had not done among them the works that no one else did, they would not be guilty of sin, but now they have seen and hated both me and my Father." (John 15:24) You cannot deny the miraculous confirmation of Jesus unless you simply refuse to consider the evidence from multiple confirmed eyewitness accounts and follow where that evidence leads. No, miracles are not possible. Unless you're God, that is. And that was exactly the point. There is nothing unintelligent about that.

### Final proof - His resurrection

With all the evidence summarized so far, there remains one more item that surpasses all else. It is the event that turned the last of the honest skeptics into lifelong believers. It is miraculous and in fact the pinnacle of the miraculous.

It is the documented, verified, unbelievable yet absolutely true, multiple witnessed resurrection of the executed Jesus.

Why does it matter? There are dozens of documented miraculous events attesting to his truthfulness in claiming to be the son of God in human flesh, and there are multiple other confirming truths as we've seen albeit in such a brief summary. Nevertheless, his resurrection (if it actually took place) stands as the ultimate and final proof. If it didn't happen, he is a fraud like no other, for he predicted it multiple times for all to hear and write down. Faith is then worthless and, as Paul observed in 1 Corinthians 15, Christians are the most pathetic of all people. But if it did happen, every single prophecy about him is finally fulfilled and he is, by irrefutable evidence, the Lord who came to bring God's ultimate love and salvation to the world. We need to know and we can know. There is no scientific experiment you can run in a lab to determine if it happened, just as there is no experiment you can run to determine who committed a murder. (Has it ever occurred to you that most of the things you believe -- that the Roman Empire existed, that your grandfather lived, that you ate breakfast this morning -- can't be scientifically proven? You study the available evidence as objectively as you can.) To consider the resurrection we should proceed just as we do with the murder in a court of law or when examining any other historical event. We examine all the available evidence and the witness testimonies, assess their credibility, apply logic and known facts to consider the likelihood of the possible explanations, and draw our conclusions as to the legal and historical truth of the matter.

**Arguments against Jesus' death**

First we must decide if Jesus actually died on the cross. That may sound strange because you probably already know that this truth is historically documented beyond all doubt. Yet there are some who cling to any number of theories which deny this. (If he didn't die then he wasn't resurrected, in which case he isn't God, in which case I can ignore him.) The various theories strain credibility to such a degree that we won't give them a great deal of discussion here, but they do serve to illustrate a point. One theory holds that Pontius Pilate was bribed to take Jesus down from the cross before he was dead. There are so many logical holes in this (not the least of them being that there is absolutely no evidence for it anywhere and that no one had any reason at all to want such an outcome) that it is largely met with derision even by people who think Jesus was a fraud and a criminal. Another theory holds that Jesus had an identical twin who was unknown to anyone but substituted for him in crucifixion. Another called the "swoon theory" holds that he was debilitated just shy of the point of death such that they thought he was dead and took him down from the cross, never realizing the mistake even as they placed him in a tomb. He then revived after a few days' rest in the tomb (without food or water, of course) to the point that he moved the massive sealing stone away, overpowered the detachment of Roman soldiers standing watch, and escaped to return to his disciples.

Among all the other absurdities in this, it's difficult to suggest that a highly trained and professional Roman execution squad, experienced in causing death and proud of it, couldn't figure out that they failed to kill this one. From a medical standpoint it's also mystifying how one spontaneously revives after a spear has been inserted into the chest cavity to tear through the lung, the heart, and probably the aorta. Even without the mountain of evidence affirming the event, these ideas are frankly just so downright ridiculous as to reek of a determination to avoid the truth at all costs. Even the members of the Jesus Seminar, among them some of the most ardent deniers of his resurrection, agree that Jesus lived and taught and very definitely died on a Roman cross.

There are several additional theories purporting that Jesus stayed dead after his crucifixion like any other mere human. They're all full of unexplainable holes and insurmountable logical discrepancies -- fatal flaws, as an attorney would rightly label them -- which make them exactly as plausible as the theories which deny his death. (These deserve so much more attention than the brief summaries here. It is really hoped that the reader may want to look further, perhaps starting with some of the excellent references included.) Of course, the stolen body theory is the oldest and most frequently heard, having been manufactured almost immediately to try to counter the bomb-

> *Even the members of the Jesus Seminar, among them some of the most ardent deniers of his resurrection, agree that Jesus lived and taught and very definitely died on a Roman cross.*

shell news of a man who didn't stay dead, just like he had predicted. The idea is that the disciples came by night and stole his body to make it look as if he had risen. The problems are obvious. How did they overpower Roman soldiers, who knew that failure to guard the tomb would result in their own execution? Since virtually all the disciples, scared to death and despondent that the one they had hoped in was apparently now dead and defeated, had fled at his crucifixion, what would now bring them back to hatch this plan? Why would they want to try to convince anyone that he had risen if they were hiding his corpse? Believing and proclaiming his mission and resurrection ruined the rest of their earthly lives and led to most of their deaths. And as noted earlier, who can believe that they accepted torture and execution without a single one of them recanting if they knew the whole time that he was never raised and they had his body? There's just no way to make it plausible in the least.

The hallucination theory is another, holding that he decomposed in the tomb like everyone else and no one even suggested otherwise. Some time later, the disciples were subconsciously overcome by their grief and perhaps guilt and disappointment over the now-dashed hope that he was going to lead them to an earthly victory. They began to hallucinate that they saw him alive, and as they told the stories to one another the idea took on a life of its own, causing other people to have the same hallucinations. Eventually the legend grew into a resurrection story and they went back and made up the details we now read in the historical accounts. The problems are numerous. We have noted the long period of time it takes for legends to arise and grow. His unexplainable empty tomb was known to all Jerusalem very immediately. (Even without TV and internet, you can imagine that news spread pretty quickly!) And his numerous appearances to many different people began at the same time, starting on the very Sunday when the tomb was found empty. This leads to the extreme improbability of multiple people all independently developing the same hallucination at the same time. And as we see in Paul's recap of the post-resurrection appearances, there was one occasion when it would have been necessary for more than five hundred people to "see" the same delusion.

> Is Jesus for real? If we honestly and critically examine the evidence, the answer can only be an emphatic and completely assured yes.

"For I delivered to you as of first importance what I also received: that Christ died for our sins in accordance with the Scriptures, that he was buried, that he was raised on the third day in accordance with the Scriptures, and that he appeared to Cephas, then to the twelve. Then he appeared to more than five hundred brothers at one time, most of whom are still alive, though some have fallen asleep. Then he appeared to James, then to all the apostles." (1 Corinthians 15:3-7)

Paul's summary list doesn't even include a number of other appearances that are recorded elsewhere. There is no plausibility here. Notice that most of these witnesses were still alive when Paul wrote this down, so had there been any doubt of the reality of what they saw it would have quickly unraveled with a few incisive questions. It further fails to explain why the apostles would have clung to such a delusion as they were killed for it. And finally we must point out that if a false story of resurrection was engendering belief in so many and ruining the power structure of the Jewish religious authorities, all they had to do was produce his dead and decomposing body, load it on a cart, and parade it through the streets and plazas of Jerusalem. It would be an immediate and deliciously embarrassing end of Christianity and any

Jesus stories forever. But they couldn't. He was raised, and everyone knew it from so many appearances and trustworthy witness accounts. As Peter notes to the assembled crowd on Pentecost, seven weeks later, "This Jesus God raised up, and of that we all are witnesses." (Acts 2:32) If he were lying, someone in that crowd of thousands would have brought out the body and shut them down. But they couldn't.

**There is only one logical conclusion**

The few remaining anti-resurrection theories don't fare any better. One holds that the women on that early Sunday morning and then his other disciples went to the wrong tomb and were thus confused. However they were the same women who had been there on Friday when he was placed in the tomb, the absence of guarding soldiers would have been obvious, and above all the first time they told such a story they would quickly have been directed to the correct tomb where his dead body still lay. And we won't even spend time discussing the theory that Jesus was actually an extraterrestrial alien with superhuman properties which allowed him to simulate death then revive and use telepathy to influence people. The fact is that all of the evidence and all logical thought are consistent with the historical accuracy of his resurrection. The secular historical records and archaeological finds confirm that it was a well documented and indisputable event. There exists no evidence that can refute it or even cast doubt upon it. None of the theories raised against it can begin to explain the empty tomb and the absence of a body, the absence of motivation for his disciples to perpetuate a lie or delusion, the multiple eyewitnesses seeing the same thing, the people who could have refuted any deception having that opportunity but becoming followers instead, his skeptical brothers becoming believers, and confused and dejected disciples very suddenly becoming bold and unstoppable crusaders with the message of a living savior. It is the same final and ultimate proof that gives assurance and hope to his followers today: "Blessed be the God and Father of our Lord Jesus Christ! According to his great mercy, he has caused us to be born again to a living hope through the resurrection of Jesus Christ from the dead, to an inheritance that is imperishable, undefiled, and unfading, kept in heaven for you, who by God's power are being guarded through faith for a salvation ready to be revealed in the last time." (1 Peter 1:3-5)

## We cannot deny - Jesus is for real

Is Jesus for real? If we honestly and critically examine the evidence, the answer can only be an emphatic and completely assured yes. In the story of his life a Messiah is born, a perfect sacrificial lamb atones for sin in his death, the king of the universe arises from the grave, and a savior calls to you. This man is no legend or lunatic. He is not history's worst liar, but the only other choice: Lord of the universe, and of our souls if we will let him. "And this is the testimony, that God gave us eternal life, and this life is in his Son. Whoever has the Son has life; whoever does not have the Son of God does not have life." (1 John 5:11-12)

He said that he came to seek and save that which was lost. He said that God loved the world so much that he wished that none should perish but have everlasting life instead. He said that no one can come to the Father except through him. What will you do with this truth?

"The name of the Lord (says the scripture) is a strong tower, hither the righteous flee and are safe (Proverbs 18:10). Let us secure His favor and He will lead us through the journey of this life and at length receive us to a better."

SAMUEL ADAMS

CHAPTER 4

# God's Plan of Salvation

BY ANDY RICHTER

GOD DESIRES THAT ALL HUMAN BEINGS fully commit their lives to Him.

In this chapter, we assume there is a God (Chapter 1), that the Bible is His inspired word (Chapter 2), and that Jesus is the Son of God (Chapter 3). God has offered salvation as a free gift for all mankind by redeeming everyone through His Son, Jesus Christ. Every competent individual must obey God's commandments to receive and retain the salvation God offers. This chapter will explain God's plan of salvation in more detail. As you read through it, you are encouraged to think about your own life and your present relationship to God Who is your Creator.

Salvation from God is not whatever you want it to be. We can only approach God on His terms, not on our terms. God is Who He is. He is not the god of our (or any human's) imagination. Study God's Word to fully understand who God is and what He expects from you. When you do, you will eventually come to the realization that God expects you to respond to His invitation of salvation. His offer of salvation is made on His terms, not ours. We cannot save ourselves.

We will start our explanation by defining several important terms based on how they are used in the Bible. These definitions are found in Strong's Bible Concordance. Please refer back to these definitions as needed.

**Christ** - *anointed one*
The term, Christ, is a title which means the anointed one. Christ was anointed as the Messiah.

**redemption** - *distinction, deliverance, ransom payment in full*
God redeemed mankind by sending his Son, Jesus Christ, to earth to live a sinless life and to freely offer Himself as a blood sacrifice for our sins.

**grace** - *gratitude, extend favor*
Grace is God offering redemption to mankind without our deserving it.

**salvation** - *deliverance, rescue, aid, to make safe, free*
Salvation describes the spiritual process we go through to claim the redemption offered by God through Jesus Christ, ultimately spending eternity with God in heaven. Salvation is conditional upon our accepting God's free gift.

**justification** - *acquittal, vindication, righteousness*
God considers us to be righteous based on our obedience to the gospel and cleansed of our sins through the blood of Jesus Christ.

**sanctification** - *state of purity, holiness*
When we are obedient to the gospel, God makes us pure and sets us apart for His service.

**holy** - *sacred, pious*
We are to be sacred or pious, just like God.

**forgive** - *pardon*
God forgives or pardons our sins through our obedience to the gospel which invokes the blood sacrifice of Jesus Christ.

**sacrifice** - *tribute, offering*
A sacrifice is the way that God prescribes for us to exchange something of value (Jesus' blood sacrifice) for something we need (forgiveness of our sins.)

**sin** - *guilt, offense, moral evil, to miss the mark*
A sin is when we do not do (miss) what God has commanded us to do (the mark).

**savior** - *deliverer, to make safe, free*
A savior is someone who delivers someone from their sins. Jesus Christ is the Savior of the world having sacrificed Himself for our sins.

**hope** - *trust, be confident or sure*
Unlike the modern use of hope which means wish, hope in the Bible means an expectation based on our trust in God's promises.

**baptism** - *to cover wholly with water, dip, plunge, immerse or submerge in water*
Baptism is the act of being immersed (fully submerged) in water to receive the forgiveness of sins and the gift of the Holy Spirit. The word literally means to dip, plunge, immerse, or submerge. Sprinkling or pouring water over someone does not fulfill God's command to be immersed in water.

    Let's start at the beginning of the world. Before God ever created the universe, He had already planned to redeem mankind by sending His Son, Jesus Christ, to be our savior. As we examine God's plan of salvation, we will observe that it is a model of consistency. Man may ebb and flow during the course of his life, but God does not change. God's nature is described in the Bible.

    "Jesus Christ is the same yesterday and today and forever." (Hebrews 13:8) "but we speak God's wisdom in a mystery, the hidden wisdom which God predestined before the ages to our glory." (1 Corinthians 2:7)

Paul gave a six-line summary of the "mystery of godliness" by incorporating into the sacred text what is thought by some to have been the words of an early Christian hymn:

"And without controversy, great is the mystery of godliness:
He who was manifested in the flesh,
Justified in the spirit,
Seen of angels,
Preached among the nations,
Believed on in the world,
Received up in glory." (I Timothy 3:16)[1]

Soon after creation, we find God beginning to reveal His plan of redemption to the earliest humans, Adam and Eve. Referring to the serpent who deceived Eve, God said,

"And I will put enmity
Between you and the woman,
And between your seed and her seed;
He shall bruise you on the head,
And you shall bruise him on the heel." (Genesis 3:15)

Enmity refers to the spiritual battle of righteousness and evil that has been ongoing throughout human history. **Every human is a part of or at the very least affected by this spiritual battle, whether or not they realize it.**

The phrase "her seed" is the earliest reference in the Bible to the eventual savior that God would send in the form of Jesus Christ.

Continuing through the Bible, we find God making several promises to Abraham to prepare the way for Jesus to enter the world.

"I will make you exceedingly fruitful, and I will make nations of you, and kings will come forth from you. I will establish My covenant between Me and you and your descendants after you throughout their generations for an everlasting covenant, to be God to you and to your descendants after you. I will give to you and to your descendants after you, the land of your sojournings, all the land of Canaan, for an everlasting possession; and I will be their God. (Genesis 17:6-8)

Abraham and his wife, Sarah, had a child named Isaac. Isaac and his wife, Rebekah, had two children, Esau and Jacob. God repeated the promise He gave to Abraham, first to Isaac and later to Jacob. God changed Jacob's name to Israel. Jacob had twelve sons, one of whom was named Judah. Many years later Jesus was born into the tribe (descendants) of Judah, thus fulfilling the promise God made to Eve in the Garden of Eden and to Abraham, Isaac, and Jacob.

God sent His Son, Jesus, to the earth to live a sinless life as a man and to offer Himself freely as a blood sacrifice for the forgiveness of sins of all mankind. To convince mankind that Jesus was the Son of God and the people should follow Him, God provided a wealth of evidence. A few examples are given below.

1) Jesus fulfilled the Old Testament prophecies of the Messiah.

One of God's prophets in the Old Testament, Isaiah, described the Messiah as a suffering servant. Isaiah 53:1-12, which was written several hundred years prior to Jesus coming to earth, includes God's entire plan of redemption.

[1] "Who has believed our message?
And to whom has the arm of the Lord been revealed?
[2] For He grew up before Him like a tender shoot,
And like a root out of parched ground;
He has no stately form or majesty
That we should look upon Him,
Nor appearance that we should be attracted to Him.
[3] He was despised and forsaken of men,
A man of sorrows and acquainted with grief;

And like one from whom men hide their face
He was despised, and we did not esteem Him.
⁴ Surely our griefs He Himself bore,
And our sorrows He carried;
Yet we ourselves esteemed Him stricken,
Smitten of God, and afflicted.
⁵ But He was pierced through for our transgressions,
He was crushed for our iniquities;
The chastening for our well-being fell upon Him,
And by His scourging we are healed.
⁶ All of us like sheep have gone astray,
Each of us has turned to his own way;
But the Lord has caused the iniquity of us all
To fall on Him.
⁷ He was oppressed and He was afflicted,
Yet He did not open His mouth;
Like a lamb that is led to slaughter,
And like a sheep that is silent before its shearers,
So He did not open His mouth.
⁸ By oppression and judgment He was taken away;
And as for His generation, who considered
That He was cut off out of the land of the living
For the transgression of my people, to whom the stroke was due?
⁹ His grave was assigned with wicked men,
Yet He was with a rich man in His death,
Because He had done no violence,
Nor was there any deceit in His mouth.
¹⁰ But the Lord was pleased
To crush Him, putting Him to grief;
If He would render Himself as a guilt offering,
He will see His offspring,
He will prolong His days,
And the good pleasure of the Lord will prosper in His hand.
¹¹ As a result of the anguish of His soul,
He will see it and be satisfied;

By His knowledge the Righteous One,
My Servant, will justify the many,
As He will bear their iniquities.
[12] Therefore, I will allot Him a portion with the great,
And He will divide the booty with the strong;
Because He poured out Himself to death,
And was numbered with the transgressors;
Yet He Himself bore the sin of many,
And interceded for the transgressors." (Isaiah 53:1-12)

2) The first four books of the New Testament, Matthew, Mark, Luke, and John, record the events of Jesus' life, including His teachings as well as the miracles He performed to convince people that His words were from God. These books are referred to as the gospels, because they contain the good news of Jesus.

"[1] Do not let your heart be troubled; believe in God, believe also in Me. [2] In My Fathers house are many dwelling places; if it were not so, I would have told you; for I go to prepare a place for you. [3] If I go and prepare a place for you, I will come again and receive you to Myself, that where I am, there you may be also. [4] And you know the way where I am going." [5] Thomas said to Him, "Lord, we do not know where You are going, how do we know the way?" [6] Jesus said to him, "I am the way, and the truth, and the life; no one comes to the Father but through Me." (John 14:1-6)

3) The remaining twenty-three books of the New Testament record how people responded to the teachings of Jesus in the first century as well as many instructions for living our lives as Jesus did.

"[38] Peter said to them, "Repent, and each of you be baptized in the name of Jesus Christ for the forgiveness of your sins; and you will receive the gift of the Holy Spirit. [39] For the promise is for you and your children and for all who are far off, as many as the Lord our God will call to Himself." [40] And with many other words he solemnly testified and kept on exhorting them, saying, "Be saved from this perverse generation!" ⁴¹ So then, those who had received his word were baptized; and that day there were added about three thousand souls." (Acts 2:38-41)

"¹ Now I make known to you, brethren, the gospel which I preached to you, which also you received, in which also you stand, ² by which also you are saved, if you hold fast the word which I preached to you, unless you believed in vain. ³ For I delivered to you as of first importance what I also received, that Christ died for our sins according to the Scriptures, ⁴ and that He was buried, and that He was raised on the third day according to the Scriptures." (1 Corinthians 15:1-4)

"²² But the fruit of the Spirit is love, joy, peace, patience, kindness, goodness, faithfulness, ²³ gentleness, self-control; against such things there is no law.'" (Galatians 15:22-23)

"⁵ Now for this very reason also, applying all diligence, in your faith supply moral excellence, and in your moral excellence, knowledge, ⁶ and in your knowledge, self-control, and in your self-control, perseverance, and in your perseverance, godliness, ⁷ and in your godliness, brotherly kindness, and in your brotherly kindness, love. ⁸ For if these qualities are yours and are increasing, they render you neither useless nor unfruitful in the true knowledge of our Lord Jesus Christ.'" (2 Peter 1:5-8)

God does not limit His offer of salvation to any particular person or group of people. God's desire is for all to be saved, no matter how good or evil a person may be at any point in his or her life.

"³ This is good and acceptable in the sight of God our Savior, ⁴ who desires all men to be saved and to come to the knowledge of the truth." (1 Timothy 2:3-4)

As you read and study the Bible which is God's Word, you may come to an understanding of what God intends for you. A proper response to God is as follows.

**Repent of your sins (Acts 2:38)**

When used in the New Testament as a command to the alien in order to (obtain) the remission of sins, it always indicates such a change of mind as produces a change or reformation of life under circumstances warranting the conclusion that sorrow for the past would or had preceded it.[2]

**Confess that Jesus is God's Son (Matthew 10:32)**

In the earlier ages of the church persons were required to confess with the mouth their faith in Jesus Christ as the Son of God prior to baptism.[3]

**Be baptized for the remission of your sins and to receive the gift of the Holy Spirit (Acts 2:38)**

When Jesus commanded the apostles to "Teach all nations, baptizing them into the name of the Father, and of the Son, and of the Holy Spirit," Matthew 28:19, there was an implied obligation upon those to whom they were sent, to submit to be baptized by them. Upon whom did this obligation rest? These may and should be baptized; none other may, unless other authority be shown for it.[4]

Baptism as it is used in the Bible means to be immersed in the water, which excludes sprinkling or pouring. This is when the penitent believer comes in contact with the sacrificial blood of Jesus Christ and makes a whole hearted life long commitment to God.

You may be thinking, what if I respond to God's call? What is next after baptism? What kind of commitment am I really making?

God expects each of us to make a full whole hearted commitment to follow Him and glorify Him for the rest of our lives. We will be a work in progress for the remainder of our days on earth, constantly growing closer to God.

Read these Bible passages for further study.

Ephesians 4:17-24, I John 1:5-7, Galatians 5:19-25, Philippians 1:27,

3:12-14, II Peter 1:2-11, Romans 6:1-19

You may be thinking, what if I don't respond to God's call? God has also addressed your situation in His Word by revealing His wrath.

"He who believes in the Son has eternal life; but he who does not obey the Son will not see life, but the wrath of God abides on him." (John 3:36)

"For the wrath of God is revealed from heaven against all ungodliness and unrighteousness of men who suppress the truth in unrighteousness." (Romans 1:18)

Or you may be thinking that you are already saved because you did something in the past and thought at the time that you were doing all that was necessary. If what you did matches what is described above, then all is well. If all you did was pray a prayer to God, or invite Jesus into your heart, or do something else that is not what was described above, then you have not followed God's plan and are subject to His wrath.

"Every man ever born was destined to be the son of God through Christ; that is, a Christian. Many do not know this, but the hunger and loneliness of countless human hearts who have not found their anchor in Christ show that man seeks in vain for any true rest in any other source than Christ. Of course, man can live against his destiny, but if he does, he is sure to be hurt. Wild geese can forsake the water courses; the tiger can renounce the jungle; the fishes can leave the sea with the same prospect of success that confronts man when he rejects the government of God and tries to walk alone.

Think for a moment on this question - "Can I really believe that God made me with such a nature that I will be happier in serving the devil than in serving God?" If, in man's thinking, any intelligence whatever is imputed to God, it is obvious what the answer must be. To ask this question in sober thought is to know the truth."[5]

"(The Bible) is the rock on which our country rests."

-ANDREW JACKSON

CHAPTER 5

# A History of Christianity

BY KEITH ERICSON

The church that Christ promised He would build was founded on the Day of Pentecost in 30 A.D. Through the remaining years of the first century the church had spread to the entire known world at that time. Throughout the first century there were strong churches and weak churches. The apostles gave many warnings to the leadership of the churches telling them what to expect from those who would harm, even destroy, the churches.

The first century church was guided by the apostles who were in turn guided by the Holy Spirit. Right before Jesus was tried and crucified He spoke to His apostles following their observance of the Passover. One point that stands out was Christ's promise of the Holy Spirit (John 14-16). When Luke wrote in Acts 2 that the believers continued in the Apostles' doctrine, he was referring to the guidance of the Holy Spirit. The apostles did not dream up God's plan, they simply followed the guidance of the Holy Spirit.

Jesus' brothers, until His resurrection, did not believe He was the Son of God. But then they became strong leaders in the church, with

James and Jude both writing letters contained in the New Testament. Jude, in his letter, confirmed without a doubt that the gospel was complete and needed nothing that could be added by man. "I found it necessary to write to you exhorting you to contend earnestly for the faith which was once for all delivered to the saints" (Jude 3). This letter was written at least thirty-five years after the church was established on the day of Pentecost.

> *The apostles did not dream up God's plan, they simply followed the guidance of the Holy Spirit.*

As mentioned above, the first century church received warnings about false teachers who would harm the church. These attacks on the church were described in plain, direct language.

The Apostle Paul, as he was finishing his third missionary journey, gave a specific warning to the Ephesian elders who met him at Miletus. He warned them that after his departing grievous wolves would cause extreme trouble for the Ephesian church. Paul wrote to Timothy, a young preacher, about the falling away. He also wrote to the churches at Thessalonica and Galatia about the falling away. Here is what he wrote to them:

To the Thessalonians – "that day (the second coming of Christ) will not come unless the falling away comes first, and the man of sin is revealed, the son of perdition, who opposes and exalts himself above all that is called God or that is worshipped, so that he sits in the temple of God, showing himself that he is God" (II Thessalonians 2:1-4).

To Timothy – "Now the Spirit expressly says that in latter times some will depart from the faith, giving heed to deceiving spirits and doctrines of demons, speaking lies in hypocrisy, having their own conscience seared with a hot iron, forbidding to marry, and commanding to abstain from foods which God created to be received with thanksgiving by those who believe and know the truth" (I Timothy 4:1-5).

To the Galatians – "I marvel that you are turning away so soon from him who called you in the grace of Christ, to a different gospel which is not another, but there are some who trouble you and want to pervert the gospel of Christ" (Galatians 1:6-9).

In the final letter in the New Testament (the Revelation, written about 95 A.D.) the Apostle John wrote to the seven churches of Asia, reprimanding five because they were in some way displeasing to the Lord (Revelation 2-3).

So there were constant warnings to the first century churches about being on guard against false doctrine and false teachers.

The primary responsibility for leading/overseeing each congregation belonged to elders whose qualifications leave no doubt about how seriously they should apply themselves to the task of teaching and guarding against error. Following are some of the qualifications:

Husband of one wife, of good behavior, able to teach, one who rules his own house well, having faithful children, not a novice, must have good testimony among those who are outside, not self-willed, not given to wine, holding fast the faithful word as he has been taught. These qualifications show how important this leadership position was and still is today. Deacons' qualifications are also spelled out. Deacons were younger men who would be servants in each congregation. (Read Titus I: 5-9 and I Timothy 3: 1-13 for the complete list of qualifications for elders and deacons.)

We must recognize this – the elders in each congregation were not dominated by one who would be more powerful or more important than his fellow elders. They were on equal footing with each other. Each congregation was completely independent from its sister congregations. This pattern is easily recognized in New Testament teaching.

It's easy to learn by reading the New Testament how the church was organized and how it worked in the first century. But major disagreements arise now when discussing how the church should be organized, and how it should have functioned up through the centuries. It is important to note that there is not one passage of scripture in the New Testament indicating that the church should change into something else as the centuries passed. There is not one passage that indicates the church can depart from the faith once for all delivered to the saints by the apostles. In fact there are constant warnings about false doctrine and false teachers.

Now we can follow the Christian religion up through the centuries to determine why some have led believers away from the teachings of the Apostles and from the teaching of the New Testament. And as we look at how the church was organized in the first century we can ask ourselves if the church in the 21st century should follow that New Testament pattern as closely as possible or should the church now follow some of the false teachings that originated as the centuries passed.

## Digression first appeared in church leadership

As elders assumed their duties a development occurred which began the digression. One elder became the prominent elder, gaining preeminence over the others in some congregations. As this feature spread, that special elder assumed the title of bishop, separating himself from the other elders. This was happening in the second century. Congregations were still independent entities but this also began to change. As time passed churches began holding conferences or conventions to decide on issues that were important to the churches. The decisions that originated with these conventions became canons or rules. The Romans began calling these conventions Councils. At first the bishops representing their local churches acted in the name of their people, but they gradually began to feel that power was given them by Christ to dictate rules of faith and conduct to the people. As the councils extended over the whole Christian world, certain "head men" were placed over the councils in different parts of the world and these men assumed the title of Patriarch. The final result, years later, was the Roman Patriarch – the Pope.

While this power system was developing the church was also digressing from the New Testament in other ways. In the third century the practice of infant baptism originated because of the feeling that infants inherited original sin. The practice of infant baptism and the doctrine of original sin both are in direct opposition to New Testament teaching. And this happened no more than two hundred years after the church was established.

Another departure from New Testament teaching happened when sprinkling or pouring took the place of immersion. This also happened in the middle of the third century. Baptism was by immersion only for believers in the first century but as we learn about the elevation of bishops and their feeling that they were acting by power given by Christ, we see the church changing into an institution separating itself more and more from the first century church. (Concerning immersion see Romans 6:4 and Colossians 2:12) Also note that the Greek word BAPTIDZO had only one meaning – immerse. (The New Testament was originally written in Greek.) Men who translated the Bible into English came up with the new word "baptize" and gave it three meanings –sprinkle, pour or immerse. Bible scholars today who promote/accept sprinkling or pouring in place of immersion must know that this is a violation of the teaching of the apostles.

## Roman Emperor Constantine has major impact

Persecutions of Christians were taking place almost constantly by the Roman government up until the fourth century when Emperor Constantine legalized Christianity. The empire was gradually weakening and the emperor realized Rome couldn't continue persecuting Christians and fighting invaders from the north. So he legalized the Christian religion. This ended persecutions but it also brought the church directly under the power of Rome. From this point on, Bible historians tell us that the New Testament church lost most of its identity - the identity of the church Christ died for and that the Apostles established during the first century.

Some of the major digressions beginning in the third century that identify the Roman church as the religious organization that supplanted the New Testament church are: (some we have already explored) – infant baptism, sprinkling or pouring instead of immersion, canonizing saints, transubstantiation (the claim that the bread and wine in the communion actually turn into the flesh and blood of Christ), claiming that the Apostle Peter was the first Pope and that all popes are successors to Peter, instrumental music in worship services, indulgences and worship of the virgin Mary.

## Transubstantiation

The idea that the bread and wine in the communion change into the actual body and blood of Christ originated no earlier than the sixth century, but early in the ninth century a monk named Radbert wrote a book in which he promoted transubstantiation. The Council of Trent in 1551 officially adopted the doctrine. There is absolutely nothing in the New Testament that would in any way support this doctrine. This is just one example of how the prophesies of the falling away would occur.

## The First Pope - - Peter?

In Matthew 16 Jesus asked His disciples who they would say He was. Peter answered that Jesus was the Christ, the Son of the Living God. A few sentences later Jesus said, "You are Peter and on this rock I will build My church". So He addressed Peter and talked to him about something else. Jesus was obviously telling his disciples He would build His church on the truth (rock) that He was the son of God. On the day of Pentecost, Peter preaching to the Jews, said that God had made that same "Jesus Whom you crucified both Lord and Christ." (Acts 2:36) The church came into existence at that time because about three thousand were baptized, having been convicted of crucifying the Son of God. Looking again at Matthew 16, the Roman church says that Jesus was telling Peter that He would build His church on Peter. Looking at the sentence structure there is no way that Jesus was telling Peter something about Peter. Instead, He was telling Peter about a specific event in the near future – that He would build His church on the truth (rock) that He was the Christ, the Son of the living God.

Peter was executed by the Romans about 67 A.D. According to the Catholic Bible for children, the first successor to Peter was a man named Linus. The Apostle John wrote five books/letters toward the close of the first century, at least twenty five years after Peter's death, and not once did he mention Linus or any of the others who supposedly followed Peter. Isn't it strange that these "spiritual leaders" were not even recognized during the closing years of the first century?

In 434 A.D. Sixtus III, bishop of Rome, announced that he exercised supreme authority over the church. This seems to be the beginning of what would become the office of Pope. However, historians tell us that the year 606 A.D. marks the beginning of the Roman Catholic church, fully organized, with the Pope of Rome as its head.

**Acceptance of instrumental music in worship**

The use of a musical instrument to accompany singing in church services did not happen until about the fifth or sixth centuries. Controversy surrounded their use with many church leaders being opposed on scriptural grounds because it was a generally accepted fact that instruments were not used in the first century church, nor was there any mention by the apostles sanctioning their use. So using instruments may have started in the fifth or sixth centuries, but historians say that the organ was used widely several centuries later. Historians also point out that while there is no use of instruments in the first century, New Testament writers did urge Christians to sing and make melody in their hearts to the Lord.

**Purgatory – After death – punishment before heaven**

Church leaders had numerous discussions about the condition of the soul after death. The idea of a place where the dead could suffer before entering heaven gradually became catholic doctrine, probably sometime after the fourth century. In 1563 at the last session of the Council of Trent the doctrine of Purgatory was finally confirmed.

**Worship of the Virgin Mary**

In order to worship the Virgin Mary as the Mother of God, she had to be declared free from original sin. Much debate continued through the centuries. Finally in 1854 Pope Pius IX declared the doctrine as a matter of faith. From that time anyone who denied the doctrine was condemned as a heretic. Catholic dogma says Mary remained a virgin throughout her life and when Jesus' brothers and sisters are mentioned, they were really His cousins.

### Indulgences – buying redemption from sin!

Indulgences were payments to the Roman church in order to receive forgiveness for sins, even future sins. The reason for encouraging this innovation become clearer when watching Pope Leo X. John D. Cox, in his book "Church History", writes, *"Pope Leo X was eager to complete St. Peter's Cathedral in Rome. A number of Papal agents were sent out to sell indulgences as a means of raising money. A man by the name of John Tetzel proved to be a super-salesman."* Cox goes on to explain that Martin Luther mainly opposed this whole system, finally posting on the door of the church in Wittenberg, Germany his 95 theses condemning the practice of indulgences.

### Papal Infallibility

When the Pope is speaking "excathedra" on matters of faith or morals he cannot be wrong. This is the doctrine of Papal Infallibility. In 1870 Pope Pius IX declared this as Roman Catholic doctrine. Related to these thoughts is the Roman Church's pronouncement that tradition is more reliable than scripture. Costerus, a popular Catholic writer, penned these words, *"The excellency of the unwritten word doth far surpass the scripture, which the apostles left us in parchments; the one is written by the finger of God, the other by the pen of apostles. The scripture is a dead letter . . . .but tradition is written in men's hearts, which cannot be altered."*

There are many doctrines and issues concerning the Roman church which we do not have space to discuss. However, John Rowe in his book, "History of Reformatory Movements" lists in the contents fifty issues which raise all kinds of questions. He covers these topics in the text of the book.

### Martin Luther leads in the Reformation movement

Martin Luther, 1483-1546, a citizen of Germany, became disillusioned with some of the practices of the Roman church, mainly because of the unscriptural practice of indulgences. Luther's parents were poor, his father was a miner and Luther was concerned that he might end up in the same occupation. His father wanted him to study law but Martin finally decided to become a monk after almost being killed by a lightning strike. He entered the Augustinian Cloister and began a very serious study to become a Catholic monk. He wrote about his dedication, *"I chose for myself twenty-one saints, read mass every day, calling on three of them every day, so as to complete the circuit every week; especially did I invoke the Holy Virgin, as her womanly heart was more easily touched, that she might appease her son. I verily thought that by invoking three saints daily, and by letting my body waste away with fastings and watchings, I should satisfy the law, and shield my conscience against the goad; but it all availed me nothing: the further I went on in this way the more I was terrified."*

Luther said later, *"If ever a monk got to heaven by monkery, I would have gotten there."* He later was given the opportunity to visit Rome and he became very excited about a visit to the *"Holy City"*. But he became extremely disappointed at what he saw in Rome. He wrote about his experience – *"Nobody can form an idea of the licentiousness, vice and shame that is in vogue in Rome. Nobody would believe it unless he could see it with his own eyes and hear it with his own ears. Rome was once the holy city, now it is the vilest. It is true what has been said, "If there is a hell, Rome must be built over it."*

Luther was still dedicated to becoming a monk, and at the age of 29 he was installed in a professorship of Theology at Wittenburg. He had heard of Tetzel, who was selling indulgences and learned that he was coming to Wittenburg. Luther decided to do something about Tetzel's abuses. He nailed his Ninety-five theses, exposing the serious problems with indulgences, to the door of the Church of All-Saints in Wittenburg and his fame spread rapidly as one who would attack injustices, even if it meant opposing Catholic practices. Luther was not completely opposed to indulgences but he recognized the abuses and had decided to do something.

From that time on, he was heavily attacked by the Catholic leadership in Rome and in his home country. Finally, he was excommunicated because he would not recant on his opposition to what he knew were injustices promoted by the mother church.

In this chapter much is left out of Luther's battles with the Catholic leadership but the final result was the organization of the Lutheran Church, although Luther, himself did not want a church established in his name. But his work resulted in the beginning of denominations across Europe including England. The reformation movement was in full swing.

**Protestant Movement Begins**

Protestant churches began forming across Europe, dropping many of the practices formed by the Roman church, but most denominations adopted practices and creeds which still were outside New Testament teaching. But this movement was definitely identified as protests against the Roman Catholic Church. When colonists began settling in the "new world", they brought their churches with them, enjoying a religious freedom which was not always the case in Europe.

**Latter part of the 18th Century - The Restoration Movement**

The reformation movement was an effort to reform the Roman Church. Although it was successful in bringing denominations into the religious world, it did not reform the Roman Catholic Church. But in the United States in the late 1700s another movement began called the Restoration Movement with the goal to go back to the church of the New Testament and discard all of the religious practices that originated with men and were outside New Testament teaching.

It's interesting that at least four men began thinking in the same direction although they did not know each other nor did they know of their efforts. As the movement progressed about five main points stood out: Recognize Christ as the supreme authority automatically doing away with human creeds and authority; a definite distinction between the Old and New Testaments; recognizing the New Testament pattern of the church; autonomy of the local church; and unity of all Christians.

The main leaders in the movement were James O'Kelly, a Methodist preacher, who was concerned about the government of the church and believed in the autonomy of the local congregation; Dr. Abner Jones, a Baptist preacher in Vermont who finally established some local congregations who practiced New Testament worship, only used the name Christian, and accepted the Bible only as their guide; Barton W. Stone, who was concerned that he had not had any kind of "experience" when he thought he had been saved. He and five other preachers established the "Springfield Presbytery" but dissolved it in about a year because they felt it was unscriptural. In 1804 they drew up a statement called "the last will and statement of Springfield Presbytery", which claimed that all churches should be independent and should use only the Bible as a sure guide to heaven.

> ...in the late 1700s another movement began called the Restoration Movement with the goal to go back to the church of the New Testament and discard all of the religious practices that originated with men and were outside New Testament teaching.

Alexander Campbell was also one who believed the Bible should be our only guide but he came into the picture a little later. His father, Thomas Campbell, came to America in 1807, and worked with the Presbyterian church in Washington County, Pennsylvania. Because of his preaching he fell out of favor with the Presbyterian Church. He and some others formed the "Christian association of Washington", and they drew up a 30,000 word document which in essence said that the New Testament should be the only authority for Christians.

In 1809 Campbell's family joined him in America. Alexander, his son, became a leader in the restoration movement, and eventually the Campbells and those mentioned earlier got together. They had many meetings and certain disagreements but finally the restoration movement reached adulthood. Infant baptism, instrumental music in the worship service, immersion as the only baptism, rejection of missionary societies and how often to observe the Lord's Supper had been major issues. The name church of Christ became the identifying mark for the church. They realized that the church in the first century was recognized by various terms but did not have a specific name. With no competing organizations a formal name had not been necessary.

We have traced the beginning of the New Testament church, the falling away, Martin Luther's efforts to reform the Roman Catholic church and finally the restoration movement which takes us back to the church of the first century which was established by Christ's apostles. It is our belief that all "Christian Churches" should follow the New Testament as their guide and reject all practices and creeds invented by men who have no authority to change what Christ and His apostles delivered "once and for all".

"The foundations of our society and our government rest so much on the teachings of the Bible that it would be difficult to support them if faith in these teachings would cease to be practically universal in our country."

-CALVIN COOLIDGE

# CONCLUSION

In conclusion, we know God exists based on the intelligent design of our universe. Some personal examples include the design required to explain our heart, eyes, lungs, chromosomes, as well as man's moral nature.

We know God exists because He has revealed Himself to man through His Word. We have both internal and external evidences that the Bible is God's Word. Archaeology continues to confirm the Bible with each new find and has yet to contradict it. Early manuscripts of the books of the Bible as well as many duplicate copies through the centuries confirm the authenticity of the Bible. Non-Christian writers inadvertently confirmed the claims of the Bible. Over the years, many have claimed that the Bible contains errors, but those claims have been disproven.

We know that Jesus Christ really is Lord, not a liar and not a lunatic. We have both Biblical and non-Biblical evidence Jesus was Who He claimed to be. Jesus is the Son of God and the Savior of the world.

God has offered salvation by grace as a free gift for all mankind by redeeming everyone through His Son, Jesus Christ. Every competent individual must obey God's commandments and thereby put faith into action to receive and retain the salvation God offers.

Turning to God means studying God's Word and understanding

that Jesus promised He would build His church and would give specific instructions to us in order to be added to the church. These specific instructions are spelled out in the New Testament several times. We have examined the history of Christianity since the Day of Pentecost when the Lord's church began.

The Apostles described the Christian life Jesus' followers are expected to live. In Jesus' last few hours before he was crucified, He told His Apostles that the Holy Spirit would guide them as they worked to spread the Lord's message.

There can be no mistake. God did not give the human race any authority to change any of the apostles' teaching. Through the centuries, well intentioned people have attempted unsuccessfully to improve upon God's Word, often causing God's disciples to practice error. Some are beginning to wonder how long God will tolerate our disobedience.

Many attempts have been and continue to be made to return to the original New Testament pattern found in the Bible. The Restoration Movement that began in the 19th century is one example of believing and practicing only what is authorized by the Bible which is God's Word.

America's Christian heritage is a testament to how God blesses those nations who follow Him. America has been drifting away from God for some time now. Watching individuals and nations turn away from God is alarming to anyone who considers God as the ruler of this universe and the ruler of the human race. It is time to turn toward God both individually and as a nation. Doing so would solve many if not all of our society's problems.

The word "Christian" in "America's Christian Heritage" probably has different interpretations by many who read this book. If we interpret "Christian" by exploring the term in the Bible, we learn God's intent as He authored the Christian religion. This book, as nearly as possible, tries to rely on Jesus' message to all those who believe in Him as the son of God.

Many of the issues our nation deals with today are/have been so politicized that this book cannot deal with them without invading the political arena and becoming entangled in party politics which probably harms the intent of this publication.

Finally---Is the word "Christian" in the term "America's Christian Heritage" no longer important? Obviously, we believe that it is important.

---

*Members of the Crieve Hall Church of Christ are interested in you and available to study the Bible with you. Please visit our website for contact information. www.crievehall.org*

## BIBLIOGRAPHY & FOOTNOTES

**CHAPTER 1**
[1] (https://en.wikipedia.org/wiki/Brights_movement).
[2] ("In the Beginning: In Conversation with Paul Davies and Philip Adams" (January 17, 2002). http://www.abc.net.au/science/bigquestions/s460625.htm.)
[3] ("Many Worlds in One: The Search for Other Universes" (New York: Hill and Wang, 2006), 176.)
• Abraham, Dr. Peter (2007). How the Body Works, Amber Books Ltd.
• National Geographic Society (2007). Body, The Complete Human.

**CHAPTER 2**
[1] Bible, New American Standard (La Habra: The Lockman Foundation 1977).
[2] Steve Rudd, "Matthew Fontaine Maury:"Pathfinder Of Sea" Psalms 8," last modified January 2, 2010, http://www.bible.ca/tracks/matthew-fontaine-maury-pathfindxer-of-sea-ps8.htm.
[3] "Matthew Maury's Search for the Secret of the Seas His Faith in the Bible Led Him to Some Great Scientific Discoveries," June 1, 1989, https://answersingenesis.org/creation-scientists/profiles/matthew-maurys-search-for-the-secret-of-the-seas/.
[4] George W. Dehoff, Why We Believe the Bible (Murfreesboro: Dehoff Publications, 1990), 49-56.
[5] Doug Powell, Holman QuickSource Guide to Christian Apologetics (China: B&H Publishing Group, 2006), 96.
[6] Jenna Millman, Bryan Taylor, and Lauren Effron, "Evidence Noah's Biblical Flood Happened, Says Robert Ballard," CBS News, December 10, 2012, http://abcnews.go.com/Technology/evidnce-suggests-biblical-great-flood-noahs-time-happened/story?id=17884533.
[7] Doug Powell, Holman QuickSource Guide to Christian Apologetics (China: B&H Publishing Group, 2006), 194-197.
[8] Josh McDowell, Evidence that Demands a Verdict: Historical Evidence for the Christian Faith (?: ?Campus Crusade for Christ, 1972), 68-70.
[9] George W. Dehoff, Why We Believe the Bible (Murfreesboro: Dehoff Publications, 1990), 60.
[10] Josh McDowell, Evidence that Demands a Verdict: Historical Evidence for the Christian Faith (?: ?Campus Crusade for Christ, 1972), 71,72.
[11] Theosophical Ruminator, "Biblical Archaeology 44: Iconium was not in Lycaonia," September 26, 2011, https://theosophical.wordpress.com/2011/09/26/biblical-archaeology-44-iconium-was-not-in-lycaonia/.
[12] Josh McDowell, Evidence that Demands a Verdict: Historical Evidence for the Christian Faith (?: ?Campus Crusade for Christ, 1972), 72.
[13] Doug Powell, Holman QuickSource Guide to CHRISTian Apologetics (China: B&H Publishing Group, 2006), 163.
[14] Garry K. Brantley, Digging for Answers: Has Archaeology Disproved the Bible? (Montgomery: Apologetics Press, Inc., 1995), 172,173.
[15] Josh McDowell, Evidence that Demands a Verdict: Historical Evidence for the Christian Faith (?: ?Campus Crusade for Christ, 1972), 66.
[16] Neil R. Lightfoot, How We Got the Bible (Grand Rapids: Baker Books, 2010) 129,130.
[17] Rob Verger, "Bible breakthrough: Scientists unlock secrets of burned Hebrew scroll," Fox News, September 26, 2016, http://www.foxnews.com/science/2016/09/22/bible-breakthrough-scientists-unlock-secrets-burned-hebrew-scroll.html#.V-iNiOVN2uo.email.
[18] Neil R. Lightfoot, How We Got the Bible (Grand Rapids: Baker Books, 2010) 131-133.
[19] Neil R. Lightfoot, How We Got the Bible (Grand Rapids: Baker Books, 2010) 133-140.
[20] "Homer in Print: The Transmission and Reception of Homer's Works," The University of Chicago Library, https://www.lib.uchicago.edu/e/webexhibits/homerinprint/preprint.html.
[21] Josh McDowell, Evidence that Demands a Verdict: Historical Evidence for the Christian

Faith (?: ?Campus Crusade for Christ, 1972), 42,43.
[22] Josh McDowell, Evidence that Demands a Verdict: Historical Evidence for the Christian Faith (?: ?Campus Crusade for Christ, 1972), 42.
[23] Neil R. Lightfoot, How We Got the Bible (Grand Rapids: Baker Books, 2010) 34.
[24] Neil R. Lightfoot, How We Got the Bible (Grand Rapids: Baker Books, 2010) 36-41.
[25] "Bodmer Papyri of John," Biblical Training, https://www.biblicaltraining.org/library/bodmer-papyri-john.
[26] Neil R. Lightfoot, How We Got the Bible (Grand Rapids: Baker Books, 2010) 120-124.
[27] Josh McDowell, Evidence that Demands a Verdict: Historical Evidence for the Christian Faith (?: ?Campus Crusade for Christ, 1972), 45.
[28] F. F. Bruce, The New Testament Documents: Are They Reliable? (Grand Rapids: William B. Eerdmans Publishing Company, 1972), 18,19.
[29] George W. Dehoff, Why We Believe the Bible (Murfreesboro: Dehoff Publications, 1990), 90.
[30] George W. Dehoff, Why We Believe the Bible (Murfreesboro: Dehoff Publications, 1990), 90-93.
[31] F. F. Bruce, The New Testament Documents: Are They Reliable? (Grand Rapids: William B. Eerdmans Publishing Company, 1972), 22-27.
[32] P. Wesley Edwards, "Bible Errors and Contradictions," Freethought Debater, December 30, 2011, http://www.freethoughtdebater.org/2011/12/30/bible-errors-and-contradictions/.
[33] Adam Clarke, Clarke's Commentary Volume II, (New York-Nashville: Abingdon-Cokesbury Press) 105,106.
[34] Dave Miller, "At What Hour Was Jesus Crucified?", Apologetics Press, http://www.apologeticspress.org/apcontent.aspx?category=6&article=4759.
[35] Menachin Posner, "How Old Was Jehoiachin? Does Chronicles Contradict Kings?", Chabad.org, http://www.chabad.org/library/article_cdo/aid/1452602/jewish/How-Old-Was-Jehoiachin.htm.

**CHAPTER 3**
[1] The Holy Bible, English Standard Version. Wheaton, IL: Crossway Publishers, 2007.
[2] McDowell, Josh. Evidence that demands a verdict. San Bernardino, CA: Here's Life Publishers, 1979.
[3] McDowell, Josh and Sean McDowell. More than a carpenter. Carol Stream, IL: Tyndale House Publishers, 2009.
[4] Powell, Doug. Holman quick source guide to Christian apologetics. Nashville, TN: Holman Reference, 2006.
[5] Strobel, Lee. The case for Christ. Grand Rapids, MI: Zondervan, 1998.
[6] Strobel, Lee. The case for the real Jesus. Grand Rapids, MI: Zondervan, 2007.

**CHAPTER 4**
[1] Coffman, J. B. (1976). The Mystery of Redemption (p. 117), Abilene, TX: A.C.U. PRESS.
[2] Brents, T.W. (1966). The Gospel Plan of Salvation (p. 236), Nashville, TN. Gospel Advocate.
[3] Brents, T.W. (1966). The Gospel Plan of Salvation (p. 249), Nashville, TN. Gospel Advocate.
[4] Brents, T.W. (1966). The Gospel Plan of Salvation (p. 393), Nashville, TN. Gospel Advocate.
[5] Coffman, J. B. (1976). The Mystery of Redemption (p. 115), Abilene, TX: A.C.U. PRESS.

**CHAPTER 5**
[1] John D. Cox, Church History Murfreesboro, DeHoff Publications, 1951.
[2] John F. Rowe, A History of Reformatory Movements, Nashville, TN: Gospel Advocate, 1957.

**CHAPTER 6**
[1] Lang, Kenneth R. "What Are the Chances of Life on Another Planet?" Tufts Now, May 6, 2016. http://now.tufts.edu/articles/what-are-chances-life-another-planet.
[2] Obergefell vs. Hodges. https://www.supremecourt.gov/opinions/14pdf/14-556_3204.pdf 6th Circuit Court of Appeals, June 26, 2015
[3] Lisciotto, Carmelo. "Hitler Youth" http://www.holocaustresearchproject.org/holoprelude/hitleryouth.html H.E.A.R.T. 2008.